To Steve,

I'll pay you the £10.00 later

Affectionate wishes,
love
Sarah
xxxxx
28 August 1984. xxxxx

HOCKEY FOR WOMEN

Hockey for Women

by
MELVYN HICKEY
(Former England Captain)

WITH A FOREWORD BY
MARJORIE POLLARD

KAYE AND WARD · LONDON

First published by
NICHOLAS KAYE LIMITED
194–200 Bishopsgate, London EC2
1962

Second edition published by
KAYE AND WARD LIMITED
194–200 Bishopsgate, London, EC2
1970

Copyright © 1962 Nicholas Kaye Limited, 1970 Kaye and Ward Limited

All Rights Reserved. No part of this publication may be reproduced, stored in a retrieval system, or transmitted, in any form or by any means, electronic, mechanical, photocopying, recording or otherwise, without the prior permission of the copyright owner.

ISBN 0 7182 0588 X

Printed in England by
LOWE & BRYDONE (PRINTERS) LTD.,
LONDON

CONTENTS

		Page
Foreword by MARJORIE POLLARD		9
Preface		10
CHAPTER I.	HOW IT ALL BEGAN	13
II.	DRIBBLING AND FOOTWORK	19
III.	THE DRIVE AND FIELDING	23
IV.	OTHER STROKES	28
V.	DODGING AND TACKLING	33
VI.	TEAM TACTICS—CORNERS	39
VII.	TEAM TACTICS—FREE HITS	47
VIII.	TEAM TACTICS—ROLLS-ON	51
IX.	GOALKEEPER	54
X.	BACKS	57
XI.	RIGHT HALF	64
XII.	CENTRE HALF	69
XIII.	LEFT HALF	73
XIV.	RIGHT WING	79
XV.	RIGHT INNER	86
XVI.	CENTRE FORWARD	90
XVII.	LEFT INNER	95
XVIII.	LEFT WING	102
XIX.	EQUIPMENT	110

Remembering my parents—
Whose interest was ever present

LIST OF ILLUSTRATIONS

PLATES

BETWEEN PAGES 48 AND 49

PLATE I. The grip for dribbling.
II. Dribbling—front view.
III. Dribbling—side view.
IV. The grip for driving.
V. The drive.
VI. The point of contact.
VII. The follow-through.
VIII. The push-scoop stroke.
IX. *Place* stick to ball.
X. A strong, powerful stroke ending in a follow-through that is low and forwards.
XI. The jab tackle.
XII. Follow-up of the jab tackle.
XIII. The lunge tackle, followed by . . .
XIV. A two-handed tackle facing opponent.

BETWEEN PAGES 80 AND 81

XV. Rolling the ball on. Feet and stick well behind line.
XVI. Hand close to ground before release.
XVII. Be ready to step on to the field of play immediately ball has been released.
XVIII. Receiving a pass from behind on the left.
XIX. Receiving a pass from behind on the right.
XX. Interception showing one handed reversed stick fielding of the ball.
XXI. Reversed stick back pass. Head over ball; short back lift.
XXII. Taking the ball from off your toe.

XXIII.	Short follow-through.
XXIV.	Reversed stick pass to right.
XXV.	Weight on the front foot throughout.
XXVI.	A short, crisp stroke with little follow-through.
XXVII.	The bully-off.

Photographs by Gordon Catling

DIAGRAMS

	Page
DIAGRAM 1. Left and right dodges	36
2. Positions at bully-off	41
3. Corners	43
4. Rolls-on	54
5. Triangular passing	84
6. Left dodge by Left inner at long corner	99
7. Passing to the space at a free hit	105
8. Off-side	107

FOREWORD

Having known Melvyn Hickey ever since she was a student at Lady Mabel College of Physical Education, it was no surprise to me that she wrote this lively, interesting and thoroughly sensible book. Neither is it a surprise that the book should prove so successful as to make this new edition a necessity, because of the consistent demand by players and coaches in many parts of the world.

Melvyn Hickey has ceased to play in international hockey, but I can recall very clearly the many times I saw her in thrilling action. Apart from the actual skill of her play, I admired her enthusiasm, enjoyment and intelligence. These characteristics shine throughout this book. They are certainly qualities to be fostered wherever hockey is played.

This carefully written book has a message to tell whether it is schoolgirls, students or players of all standards who read it. They too will enjoy it and, at the same time, benefit from the lessons so crisply given.

Knowledge is recorded experience and certainly Melvyn Hickey has used her wide and varied experience to produce this book, now in its revised and second edition.

MARJORIE POLLARD

PREFACE

There has been much change in the years that have elapsed since the first edition of *Hockey For Women* was published in 1962. Changes not only in the game itself and in the rules that govern it, but changes also in the theory of the game, in the minds and thinking of the people who are concerned with the administration of the game and, of course, in the minds of the players too, who are, after all, the people most in direct contact with the game.

Changes, of course, will naturally occur in the normal development of things, but perhaps, when we look back at these years later, we will realise that these were the years when a whole new attitude to the game, and indeed to many sports, steadily bubbled its way to the surface.

Some may think change is a bad thing; others may welcome it. The wise will assess it and either reject or accept it on the basis of that valuation.

Of course the basic skills, both physical and mental, talked about in the chapters that follow will never change and most of this second edition therefore is unaltered. The only thing that I have tried to add, and note that I do not say substitute, is an attitude of mind that allows even more freedom, and one that is even more flexible to the sometimes rigid confines of orthodoxy that we knew before. It is an exciting thought. I have always said that there are many things—and thank heaven there are—that are neither black nor white, neither right nor wrong, but are greyed by the initiative and imagination and enterprise of the player. Nowadays there are even more. That's the only difference.

Allied to this is a way of thinking that is more professional than in past years. Do not think by this I mean for one moment that we have lost any of the sportsmanship or any of the great 'camaraderie' that exists between women hockey players all over the world, which is quite unique to our game and which must surely be the envy of many other sporting associations.

You have only to visit an international Tournament and Conference of our International Federation of Women's Hockey Associations to know that this indefinable quality which links women's hockey playing countries, regardless of colour or religion or customs or language, is stronger than ever.

Hockey is an amateur sport and as long as it is we will be safe from the sort of evils that have turned football, for instance, into something which is no longer a sport but a business.

But within our amateurism we can get, and I believe must get, a more professional approach. If England is to remain in her position as leader in the world of women's hockey, she must not only keep up but go ahead of her contemporaries. She cannot afford to rest on her laurels any longer. Very soon she will have no laurels to rest on and the fault will be no-one's but her own.

England's international opponents have improved beyond recognition. They have now learnt the game. Let us recognise that. They have a great deal that can now be learnt from them and it would be a sad thing if our great players of today in England were not given every opportunity to add to their already successful and established game.

Add is the important word here. What the players had before was pretty good—it taught the rest of the world—and there is no need to scrap it. Perhaps an adaptation here and there, but what they need now are *added new* tactics, new ways of looking at a problem, new ways of dealing with it, new ideas, an ever-constant awareness of the situation, a thought ever uppermost in their minds—how to WIN. For I personally think that is the whole aim of the game. To win well, skilfully, by physical and mental effort, fairly and within the laws of amateurism.

I think that if it is remembered that change can be either good or bad, but that good change is progress, all will be well.

The following chapters will, I hope, help you, the player, to improve and therefore to enjoy your game even more than you do now. Nothing is more satisfying than to beat a player by *good play*, when you can pat yourself on the back and say to yourself 'I did that well'. Compare that with the goal scrambled in after a mistake, or the goal saved because of bad play on your opponent's part. That's not the sort of hockey to enjoy and to be proud of, it's not even worth considering. But just remember that you, the player, and you only, CAN GET BETTER if you really want to. It's up to you.

MELVYN HICKEY
Old Rope Walk,
Sunbury-on-Thames.

CHAPTER I

HOW IT ALL BEGAN

THE origin of hockey appears uncertain. It is possible that the game derives from 'hurley' which we know was being played in Ireland as far back as 1272 B.C. On the other hand it seems equally likely that the stick game of the ancient Persians was subsequently acquired by the Greeks who in turn handed it on to the Romans and that they brought the game to our islands with their invasion. Admittedly it was a very crude form of stick game but a sculpture in bas-relief discovered in 1922 which formed part of a Greek wall built nearly 2,500 years ago does show six youths in action and two in particular taking part in a 'bully' bearing a remarkable resemblance to that of our game today except that their hooked sticks are pointing downwards instead of upwards. Then again most of the Indian tribes in America are known to have played a type of stick game but it is unlikely that this bears much resemblance to modern hockey.

Whatever the source of hockey, it is certain that it has been played for a very long time, sufficient, in fact, for it to be claimed as the oldest game in the world.

But what of women's hockey? Well that has been played for a comparatively short time. Just over eighty years ago the men hockey players in England formed 'The Hockey Association' in 1886. At that time the sporting activities of women were, to say the least, restrained and it would not have been considered at all ladylike for a young lady to run around a hockey pitch with a stick and a ball. Nor indeed had she wanted to, would it have been physically easy for her, being encumbered with yards of stiffened petticoats and skirts around her ankles. There were, however, a few who did want to and who rebelled. Already having tasted the joys of freedom, in so much as their skirts allowed, by surreptitiously joining in the men's games at great risk of punishment from their Victorian parents and, of course, tolerant suffering from their menfolk, they determined to start their own game. It didn't take them long although there must have been many gasps of horror, much criticism and little encouragement.

The very first Club to be formed in this country was Molesey, in 1887. Their leader and captain then was Miss Piper, later Mrs D'Oyly who subsequently played for England as well as Surrey and the South. They obviously had a good start. But their enthusiasm spread and nearby in Ealing another Club was formed, followed very shortly by Wimbledon. Of these three clubs only Wimbledon now remains and although today the names of Ealing and Molesey clubs are to be seen on the local fixture lists they are not related in any way to those first few pioneers. Wimbledon then is proud to be the oldest existing Club in the country and I as a proud member can vouch that enthusiasm is as high now as ever it must have been in those first pioneering days.

These three Clubs then, together with a group of keen young students at Lady Margaret Hall and Somerville College at Oxford, constituted the total number of players in the early 1890s over eighty years ago.

In Ireland, however, they had beaten us to it, for there the students at Alexandra College in Dublin had formed an Irish Ladies' Hockey Union—a great and wise step forward—and in 1894 they invited their student friends from Newnham College Cambridge (to whom the fever had now spread) to go over to play. They did, drawing three of their matches and losing one. On their return the students from Newnham determined to follow the example of their Irish friends and to form a national association so that international matches could be played. The news was spread around the few clubs and colleges and all were informed that an international match was to be played against Ireland. So it was that Miss E. G. Johnson, a member of Molesey Ladies' Hockey Club held a trial match at Neasden, selected a team and at Brighton on 10th April, 1895, an 'English' team marched out for the very first time on to the field to play 'Ireland' the latter being comprised solely of Alexandra College students. The result was a draw, neither side scoring.

But if the result produced no goals it produced something far greater, something that started the history of our Association. Immediately after the match whilst all concerned were fired with enthusiasm a meeting took place in a Brighton tea shop at which it was decided to form a Ladies' Hockey Association. That was the first and great step. Seven months later on 23rd November, 1895, the consolidation took place and the first formal meeting of the Ladies' Hockey Association was held in the Westminster Town Hall, the President elected being Miss Faithfull. Application was made to the Men's Hockey Association to accept their affiliation but no such acceptance was forthcoming—how ungallant!

Nothing daunted, however, the small but tremendously keen group carried on, changed the title from 'Ladies' to 'Women's and the now familiar A.E.W.H.A. (All England Women's Hockey Association) was well and truly on its way. Within ten years the formation and successful running of the system as we have it today of territorial, county and club hockey was in full force. After that, not only were international games played against Ireland but Scotland, Wales and Holland too and in 1914 a touring team to Australia and New Zealand set out and returned—to war in Europe—having won twenty-two of their twenty-six matches.

During the war there were other things of more importance but it was inevitable with such a determined and successfully established association that it should continue the very moment it was able to do so after the First World War. So in 1920 the first series of territorial matches was played in The Old Deer Park at Richmond and the next year a touring team was sent to the USA. There followed visits to South Africa, Germany, Holland, Belgium, Australia and the USA again and not surprisingly perhaps, after such globe trotting, the idea occurred to Mrs Heron Maxwell, the President of the A.E.W.H.A., that there should be a federation of all the Women's Hockey Associations.

In 1927 this idea was fulfilled and the I.F.W.H.A. (International Federation of Women's Hockey Associations) was formed. In domestic affairs things were happening rapidly; films and literature appeared, coaches were in great demand, the number of affiliated clubs and schools was steadily rising and everyone was interested and wanted to improve.

Again war interrupted and again the Association temporarily 'rested'. But it was so firmly established, its roots being the principles of those first few pioneers that have now become our traditions, that again as soon as they were able they showed that enthusiasm was higher than ever. They hardly needed an excuse for celebrations, but in fact 1945 was the fiftieth anniversary of that first Brighton tea shop meeting. In 1946 England entertained Scotland at Trent Bridge, Nottingham, and the followers at international matches were becoming so large that the Oval was no longer big enough to hold them and in 1951 the first match was played at Wembley—that name that now is the mecca of women's hockey in this country.

In 1953 the I.F.W.H.A. held its fourth triennial Tournament at Folkestone, and England after three years of hard work, saving, and intense organization welcomed her guests from eighteen other countries. It was indeed a happy, beneficial, binding step in the history of the hockey playing countries of the world. Three years later Australia had the honour of being hostess country and three years after that in 1959 it was the turn of Holland. Now this colourful and cosmopolitan tournament, which is almost like our own Olympic Games, is held every four years instead of three and in 1963 it took place in Baltimore, USA and in 1967 in Leverkusen, Germany.

So our hockey flourishes, at home and abroad, so our record

crowd at Wembley is broken each year, so schools and clubs and colleges, counties and territories play their games, safe and sure in the knowledge of an established, sound and hard working association behind them, nurtured and shaped from that first meeting in a Brighton tea shop. Hockey has certainly come a long way since those early days.

HOW DO I GET INTO THE ENGLISH TEAM?

I remember a stupid sort of vague dream—a day dream—that one day I would be watching some big important match, perhaps an international. I would be sitting very near to the side line and suddenly a player would be hurt or the wing would break her stick and I would be there (I would have my stick with me of course) and step into the breach and play the greatest game of my life coming off the field victorious with the roar of excited crowds ringing in my ears. It was a foolish dream, a typical dream, and yet you see not so improbable— not that my climb up to the English team was executed in quite such a nonchalant or romantic manner! But maybe you have a dream too and maybe it is worthwhile, you never know.

I said climb a minute ago because that's really what it is—a long and strenuous climb up a ladder that starts with hockey at school and ends with hockey at Wembley. So take heart if you're in your school team for you've made the first step—you are already on the first rung. Perhaps whilst you're still at school you'll get a chance to. play for your Junior County XI—the best of all the school players, but if not, then join a Club as soon as you leave and this will enable you to attend the County Trials for the Senior County XI. So club hockey is the second rung and County hockey the third.

If you are in the County XI you will attend every year just after Christmas one of the inter-county Tournaments at which are chosen the five territorial teams—North, South, East, West and Midlands. That's a hard and strenuous week and if your name is read out at the end of it then you may well be proud— the goal is in sight! But the hardest step of all is to come. Some of the best hockey in this country is played during a busy three weeks in February when all the five territories play each other and the England selectors are hard at work conferring and watching. Then at tea after the final match there is an air of expectancy and a hush falls over the room. Out of fifty-five first class players the honoured eleven are about to be read out —the proud eleven who will walk out on to the turf in their white blazers and red shorts and play to represent their country. I've been lucky, I've been one of those. You never know, you might be one, too.

CHAPTER II

DRIBBLING AND FOOTWORK

DRIBBLING is running with the ball under control. The important word here is control. You must be able at any time to pass the ball or dodge or swerve at a second's notice and that is only possible if the ball is continually at the end of the stick and not two or three yards away from it. Dribbling is really only a series of small taps at the ball as you run; you tap it enough to propel the ball forwards at the required speed but not enough to lose control of it, that is, to lose possession of it. For dribbling means possession of the ball and you, the player, and you only, are responsible for it and what it does and where it goes.

There are times of course when one can dribble in safety with longer taps than at other times, when there is plenty of room in which to work and no likelihood of being tackled but even then the ball must be under control and the player must always know and feel confident that she can make it do what she wants it to do—in other words she is the boss and not a slave to the ball. Think of the wonderful and exhilarating sight of a forward, in possession of the ball, dribbling her way, weaving in and out of opponents with the ball looking as if it were literally glued to the end of her stick. Those of you who have watched Valerie Robinson, one of England's great ball players, weave her way so compactly and so accurately through the opposition, will know what I mean. If you could dribble the ball like that and have complete confidence about it—for confidence plays a large part in this—then you too would have mastered the art of dribbling a hockey ball.

First of all see that your hands are in the right position on your stick. They should be apart and comfortable—you cannot expect to do anything successfully if you are in an uncomfortable position and dribbling is after all just a natural flowing running action, with your stick feeling and looking a part of you and you master of it.

Pick up your stick in your left hand holding it right at the top of the handle and rest it on the ground in front of you so that it points away from you. The palm of your left hand will be facing to the right and the forefinger and thumb will make a V on the top of the handle as you look down. Now place your right hand on the handle about three or four inches below and see that the 'V' formed by the thumb and forefinger of that hand is in line with the other. Look down at your stick and notice that the flat surface of the blade is facing to the left. Since you will not want the ball to go in that direction and neither will you want to move sideways in 'gallop' steps all you have to do is, without altering the position of your hands, to turn the stick to make the blade face forwards. Now the *back* of your left wrist is facing forwards, so is the palm of your right hand and so is the blade of your stick. (Plate i) Hold your stick out away from you in an almost vertical position making a space between you and your stick—not stiffly but enough to make sure that when you are dribbling, the ball is well away from your feet. Most people prefer to dribble with the ball not immediately in front of them but slightly to the right, but you must find for yourselves the most comfortable position for you where you can obtain maximum control—it will be approximately in front of the right foot (Plates. ii and iii).

The space in between your hands too is again a matter of personal choice. I find I usually have about four inches of handle showing between my hands but you must experiment until you find the position that neither causes you to bend too low thus limiting your range of vision and your running action nor too high causing you to have a weaker control over your stick. Curl the fingers of the left hand round the handle and spread those of the right hand out a little, if you feel that gives you more control of direction. Now as you run with the ball turn lots of corners, make it go where you want it to go and remember the back of that left hand leads the way and is facing in that direction all the time. Keep your eyes on the ball all the time, be ready for any bumps or obstructions (like an opponent's stick) so that you can deal with them quickly and effectively and keep your head over the ball. Your running, as I have said, is a natural action with your feet and shoulders facing forwards.

FOOTWORK

In all the techniques and skills of hockey, good footwork plays such an important part that we must now consider it more fully.

All good players have good footwork—they must have to be good players—for no matter how skilful they are with their sticks it is essential that they have as much control over their feet. This means training one's feet—getting them used to sudden stops and starts, balancing the body in many different positions and providing bursts of speed.

A considerable amount of our hockey in this country, especially our territorial and international matches, is, unavoidably, played at the worst time of our season when heavy grounds make great demands on our feet and leg muscles.

I believe one of the greatest assets in the game, and in many other games, is the power of **acceleration**. I cannot stress this too much, particularly for forward play.

I shall always remember the first big match I ever went to watch when I was still at school. It was at the Oval and I was privileged to see that great England forward Mary Russell-Vick in action. I remember the English forward line moving down the field in one line and then suddenly, as if shot from a rocket, Mary sprinted ahead on to the ball. One moment she was with the line, the next she was several paces ahead and increasing the lead. It seemed so incredible to me that I remember I glanced back at the line—yes it was still running! I have always thought what a very valuable asset it was to that team.

You may say, 'But that's a gift—otherwise we would all be international sprinters'—true enough but take heart when I say that I am confident that each one of us can IMPROVE on our sprinting and footwork. So very often it is completely neglected and we expect our feet to suddenly adapt themselves to this new exertion without any preliminary practice and training.

Practise, without a stick or a ball, running and sprinting alternately. Make the running an easy jog-trot, then suddenly sprint for a few yards slowing down to a slow run again. Gradually increase the sprinting distance as you get better and your muscles get used to the idea until you can sprint easily for twenty-five to thirty yards. Really use your feet and try to feel them pushing you forward at each step—and remember sprinting is the fastest you can possibly go. You will need that sprint if you are a wing to save the long pass that is sent ahead for you and to beat the opposition to the ball, so too if you are an inside forward to spring on to the centres from your wings, and even in halves and backs in timing your moment to intercept or tackle. Learning to *pace* yourself and your game is an important feature and might make all the difference between losing or winning. Quick mental reaction is not enough; you must have the physical power to carry it out—and don't forget —LEARN TO ACCELERATE!

To sum up: (i) Hands apart
              (ii) Stick down
              (iii) Feet and shoulders facing forwards
              (iv) Ball close to stick and away from feet
              (v) Head over ball
              (vi) Natural, balanced running action

CHAPTER III

THE DRIVE AND FIELDING

THE DRIVE

HOCKEY is two things: it is a ball game and it is a team game. It is obvious, therefore, that the pupil in acquiring the various skills and strokes must very quickly in the early stages learn to combine with the other members of her team. A player who is able to hit or drive the ball smoothly and accurately at any time in any direction is certainly a most valuable member of that team. In this chapter we will deal with the drive stroke in detail.

Pick up your stick again with the left hand first at the top of the handle. Put the right hand on as before and then slide it up to meet the left. Both hands are together and comfortable, both 'v's again in line with each other (Plate iv). This time there is no need to turn your stick to face forwards. If you glance down at the blade it is in the perfect position to hit the ball away to your left. Your left shoulder is pointing in the direction in which you wish to send the ball, the back of your left wrist is also facing that way, and the palm of your right hand is BEHIND the handle ready to add punch to the stroke. Swing your stick in front of you comfortably, moving your arms from the shoulders and just letting the blade brush the ground in front of you each time (Plate v). It's exactly like the pendulum of a clock, rhythmic and flowing, your weight transferring from your right to left foot, or from the back to the front foot, at each swing. If you place a ball in front of you between your feet you should be able to hit it quite smoothly.

But it will not go very far unless you add that punch from the right hand at the point of contact (Plate vi). It is a difficult thing to get and yet still retain the flow of the stroke but unless it happens there will be no power behind the drive. Move the ball opposite your left foot and notice that even that slight alteration in position means more weight behind the stroke and then progress to standing a little way away from the ball and stepping to it with the left foot as you make the stroke. See that you have got your head down well over the ball watching it closely and that your follow through is forwards and low (Plate vii). If your weight is transferred correctly it should be and there will be no danger of your giving 'sticks'. It is important to follow through *forwards*—so often we see beginners wrapping their sticks round them looking as if they are scything grass rather than hitting a hockey ball. Even the 'golfers' commit less of a crime for at least the pathway of their swing is correct! If you do find that you are still giving 'sticks' at the end of your stroke the fault probably lies in your wrists—keep them firm. Again if you find you are constantly raising your stick too high at the beginning of the stroke lessen the movement in the wrist joints and lift your right elbow upwards, not awkwardly but enough to prevent your stick coming above your shoulder.

Now for a word about timing. I've already mentioned the punch that must be added by your right hand. This must come just at the point of contact—not before, not after. If it is too soon you will probably hit the ground instead of the ball and if it is too late it will affect the pathway of your swing with the result that you will rapidly become a scyther.

The left hand plays an important part in all this. This is the guiding hand, the controlling hand, used to maintain the correct pathway of the swing and to steady the extra effort given from the right hand. It is all a smooth, almost relaxed, stroke of the ball sending it firmly and accurately along the ground in the desired direction. It is almost a 'knack' and when once acquired is seldom, if ever, lost. I have known players who have become perfectly good natural hitters of the ball and as soon as they began to analyse their stroke it became disjointed and unreliable. So don't think about it too much—just consider the following points and then go away and enjoy hitting the ball. That is the important thing—to enjoy it. Not that I am saying it is all easy—heaven forbid, for surely the enjoyment comes from the conquering of the challenge, the mastering of the skill? So do not go away with the idea that if it is difficult you pack up your bag and go home. There are some of us who find it all much easier than others and there are some who find it all much harder but keep the correct aim in sight all the time:

(i) Hands together
(ii) Sideways to your target
(iii) Pendulum swing
(iv) Step to ball
(v) Head over ball
(vi) Transference of weight
(vii) Follow through forwards and low

FIELDING

You will probably be practising your driving with a partner and as she hits the ball to you, you will have plenty of opportunities to improve upon your fielding.

It is as important in the game of hockey to be able to field the ball as it is to drive it or do anything else with it. Unless your team-mates feel confident that on receiving the ball you will be able to do something constructive with it, they will be reluctant to send it to you in the first place.

You have probably discovered that even on a good ground if you hold your stick out rigidly to the ball it will most probably bounce straight off it again. The whole aim of fielding is to gain control and possession as quickly as possible. The solution is to 'give' with your stick and arms as you field the ball; in other words you offer a pliable resistance instead of a rigid one.

It is exactly the same as when you catch a hard ball in cricket or rounders; you reach out and pull your hands in with the ball. So with your stick. Reach out for the ball, with your hands apart to give you maximum control, watch it carefully and as the ball touches the blade give back with your stick a little and relax your arms whilst still retaining a firm grip. The ball should still be there at the end of your stick and there should be hardly any noise in the act of receiving it. It is now ready under control for you to pass or dodge or dribble. Always have your stick down in good time as the ball comes towards you and always see that you have moved behind in line with the ball—not just your stick but your feet also. Get your partner to hit or roll balls to either side of you and practise moving to get your feet and stick behind the ball before you field it.

When you can do that well and only then can you practise fielding it with a reversed stick.

Thank goodness nowadays we have at last convinced umpires and coaches that we are not always going to obstruct an opponent if we turn our stick over and field a ball on our non stick, i.e. left, side with a reversed stick. It took a long time for this technique to be acknowledged in our game in England, although some continental teams and other international sides we played were obviously using it with great success. The poor English forward, so used to passing an opponent by using her non-stick side, was suddenly frustrated when a nonchalant and sometimes one-handed reversed stick shot out to the ball, neatly fielded it and she was left running ahead with nothing but surprise!

Of course this stroke *can* cause obstruction and it needs much practice to perform it well. Even more so if you are using it as a tackle rather than an interception. Men hockey players have used it for a long time and the Pakistani and Indian players are masters of the art.

Practise first of all in twos fielding the ball on your left with a reversed stick. Get the 'toe' of the stick in the right position, keep both hands on the stick and try to keep the shoulders facing forwards as much as possible. Then teach yourself to do two things. They are both follow-ups of the reverse stick fielding of the ball. The first is, having stopped the ball, immediately run your feet to the left behind the ball. The less time you take to do this the better. It may make all the difference between obstructing or not. The other follow-up is to tap the ball with your reversed stick, using the toe of the blade, to your right in front of your feet, so that it can be played in the normal way. The whole idea in both is that the reversed stick action is done quickly and neatly. You can then go on to trying to stop the ball with your left hand only on the stick on your non-stick side with the blade reversed (see plate xx); again speed in the resumption of a normal fielding and dribbling position is what matters. Then see if you can do it without obstructing an opponent. Remember obstruction is preventing your opponent from playing the ball.

A good practice to help your control of the ball with a reversed stick is just to find a line on the pitch and dribble the ball, slowly at first, feet running along the line but making the ball cross the line in short zig-zag passes, only 7 or 8 inches either side of the line. Just to keep up your dribbling technique you can do the opposite—keep the ball on the line and move your feet either side. A good body swerve is a very useful asset in crowded company. I hasten to add—to elude, not to obstruct, opponents!

What is important in all your reversed stick play is that you do not *substitute* it for normal fielding but *add* it to your repertoire to be used when necessary. It should *not* be a sign of laziness, but one of good judgement and skill.

CHAPTER IV

OTHER STROKES

THE PUSH STROKE

THIS is the stroke that is so useful that it tends to be overused. It is so quick, so neat, the ball can be sent so smoothly and so sympathetically that some players rapidly become eternal pushers and never hit the ball. Don't fall into this trap. It is very easy to do so—but always remember that there is a time and place for every stroke and the good player is able to assess the correct time and place—when to push and when not to push.

In the first place the stroke should only be used on a good ground, not just an even ground, but a dry and fast ground. It is no earthly good going through the motions of an athletic looking push pass terminating in a dramatic kneeling-cum-lunging position of the body if the ball sticks in the mud on its way to its destination. That is the time to hit and to hit hard! On the other hand how often does one see, especially in men's hockey, a player hitting a ball with full force to another on a good pitch when the distance to be covered is a mere few yards and the poor recipient is expected to recover from the blast in time to do something with the ball before he is tackled and loses it again. *Then* is the time for a sympathetic, firm, accurate push stroke directed as efficiently as if serving the ball on a plate—what more can one do? This is how it is done.

The hands are apart, as for dribbling. The ball is in front of you and you step up to it with the left foot as the stroke is made (Plate ix). The moment of contact must coincide with the transference of your weight and the maximum thrust from your right hand behind the handle so that all three factors combine in a throwing action (Plate x). From the point when your stick touches the ball the power must get stronger in order to propel the ball forwards. Don't let the power come before, otherwise the ball will merely trickle away. The timing, therefore, is very important, and will only come with practice. Again it is almost a 'knack' and when you have felt the weight of the ball once or twice against the stick you will get to know the exact time to make your effort. The strength comes from your wrists and arms and a lot of your body weight goes into the stroke which results in a follow through that is low and very forward, hence that almost kneeling position at the end of the stroke (Plate xi).

The amount of power behind the stroke will vary of course according to the distance required for the ball to travel. If you are really good you should be able to push the ball in hockey as accurately as a golfer putts on the green. One almost gets the feeling of 'turning off' the power when sufficient has been used to send the ball the required distance. That is why the stroke can be described when done skilfully as sympathetic.

When men players use the stroke you will probably note a difference. They usually perform the stroke much more from the side than from the front, possibly because their wrists are stronger, and can perform the movement without the aid of so much body weight behind them. I have seen some women players do it like this but not many and I think when you are practising it is much better to stand behind the ball and face it squarely before making the stroke. England's famous forward, Denise Parry, is a fine exponent of this stroke and illustrates how well one can direct the game with this accurate feeding of the ball to other players. It's a stroke that not only looks good, but inspires confidence in one's team and often demoralises opponents—very useful!

THE PUSH-SCOOP

This is my favourite stroke—although I sometimes wonder if the recipients of my endeavours are quite as pleased as I am! Usually they manage to deal with them very well which is certainly no credit to me.

The push-scoop, as its name suggests, is not merely pushing the ball but scooping, or lifting it, at the same time. It is done with exactly the same movement as the push stroke only the blade of the stick is slanted and placed under the ball at the point of contact. The whole thing is done with possibly more thrust and more follow through but this is again dependent entirely on how far it is required for the ball to travel.

Since I use it frequently for a shot at goal I am often not interested in how far the ball is going—the farther and harder the better, the one aim being to get it into the back of the net as quickly as possible. This is the shot that goalkeepers dislike most—I think all would agree about that. The ball is travelling at knee or thigh height and is most difficult to control either with pads, hand or stick. The other occasion when I use it is usually a pass right across the goal mouth from the left wing.

Here again I confess I do not generally consider where it is going to land as long as it makes possible openings for my inside forwards to score. They should of course control it first before shooting and therefore unless there are other players' sticks obstructing the way it would possibly be more advantageous to make the ball travel along the ground rather than in the air.

The real advantage of it is, as in the push stroke, that there is very little preparation necessary—one's hands remain just as they are for dribbling or controlling the ball—and therefore little warning to one's opponents and a time-saver to one's own team. You must remember that the more quickly things are done, *with understanding*, the better game you are playing. If you have very strong wrists, and I am fortunate for I have, you can get as much power into your push-scoop shot as in a drive. Remember though, as a shot this is good, as a pass it must be used with consideration.

THE FLICK

Remembering that the best dodge when about to be tackled is to *pass* the ball, there are occasions when a quick flick of the wrists with the hands remaining apart is all that is necessary to pass the ball from one player to another.

The ball does not travel very far in this stroke and must not be used when it is meant to. It is merely a quick movement of the stick where accuracy and timing are more important than power. Again there is absolutely no preparation—the stroke is, and should be, made at a second's notice—so that the direction of the shot can be delayed to the very last minute thereby wrong-footing your opponent and giving her no chance to anticipate your actions. It is not a hit at the ball since there is no back lift of your stick but merely a flick at it that follows straight on from your dribbling. Inside forwards finding themselves close together in attack, a half and forward at a roll-on and from defence to forward, when the distance is but a couple of steps will find it useful. You will get to know, if you are always aware of your own team players immediately around you when it can be used successfully and when it cannot.

REVERSED STICK

We have already discussed the reversed stick fielding of the ball. There is, of course, just as much demand for a reversed stick passing of the ball, used when it is impossible to get the feet into the right position for a normal hit, or if there is little time to do so, or perhaps merely to out-position, or wrong-foot an opponent.

A left wing or left inner who has darted into the space towards the goal line in the shooting circle will find it very helpful to be able to send a reversed stick pass across or back to her forwards. In mid-field play too a back pass or a very crisp and direct square pass between two players can prove very successful.

You must practise this a lot. Have the ball in front of you close to your feet. Make sure your head is well over the ball. With hands apart make a short back lift and a crisp hit to the right. The stick is almost vertical. A lot of power comes from the wrists with the right hand not only guiding but controlling the pathway of the stroke. As in the drive, it is a straight, not a circular, route that the stick takes and there is little follow-through. Practise it standing still first of all, and then try adding it on to a slow run. Make sure you are well up to the ball before you make the stroke.

There are occasions when the stroke is really no more than a flick. You may be racing for the ball faced by an oncoming opponent. A quick pull to the left just as her stick reaches for the ball must be followed by an equally quick reverse stick stroke, to keep the ball in play or in order to gain control of it. This is not the left hand dodge, about which I shall be talking later, and must not be confused with it. A dodge is done when in possession of the ball under full control. This reversed stick stroke is an emergency stroke performed as a last resort in order to gain possession of the ball. Or perhaps you are a left wing and, although a fast runner, as you should be, your opposing right half is a match for you and the only way to elude her, when she is in hot pursuit and there is no time to centre the ball, is to suddenly reverse her stick, stop the ball and whilst the half runs on, to get her centre in hard and quickly. Here again, you see, it is an emergency stroke. So too, if the left wing finds herself having dribbled the ball too near the goal line with not enough time or space to get herself round to centre the ball in order to save it going off the goal line, she can only reverse her stick and flick it to her right instead. Here she will have to use strength and she will need very strong wrists and a great deal of skill to perform it successfully. Not many left wings are capable of this and, it would certainly be better if they always tried to avoid finding themselves in this difficult position.

In all use of the reversed stick, the player should be very conscious of avoiding any obstruction with her body by placing herself between her opponent and the ball in performing the stroke.

CHAPTER V

DODGING AND TACKLING

I WILL repeat, since it is so important, that the best dodge of all is to pass the ball. When this is not possible because there is no one in a suitable position to receive it or better placed than yourself, it becomes necessary to elude an opponent but still retain possession of the ball. This is dodging and the quicker and more controlled way in which it is done the more skilful the player.

There are several ways of dodging a player. Dodging really amounts to anticipating what the opponent is going to do and then doing something to counteract it. A dodge, if it is to mean eluding a player, can be made simply by a body swerve without even losing contact with the ball. It is a sort of 'selling a dummy' as in rugby football. To the spectator it almost looks as if nothing has happened and one wonders how the poor tackler could have been so foolish—but what really happens is slightly more complicated. It's a trick, it's very satisfying and the more skilfully it is performed the more satisfying it is; that's the same with most things. Practise with an opponent, get her to advance towards you and then see if you can be clever enough to pretend to go one way to make her quite sure that you really are going that way, so that she is wrong footed when you change direction. Try it without a stick or ball first of all—just running, and see how you get on! Remember you can't turn your back, it is just a swerve and looks very good!

THE RIGHT DODGE

Practise this in twos. Dribble up to your partner (who is standing still in the early stages) and without altering the position of your hands on your stick when you get a yard's distance away from her push the ball diagonally to the right (her non-stick side), run past her on the left and meet up with the ball the other side of her and continue dribbling straight ahead.

When you have done this three or four times and you know what you are doing get her to move forward steadily as you approach. The dodge must now be performed earlier but the push to the right need not be so strong or far since as she is moving in the opposite direction you will be able to collect the ball the other side of her earlier. Then get her to tackle and now is when you must discover the correct timing for your dodge—the *exact* moment when to avoid her stick as you see it coming to the ball. Not too soon otherwise she has time to alter her tackle, not too late or her stick will reach the ball first. All dodging is a matter of timing and control. It is important in practice to really continue dribbling on after the dodge—it is only half completed if you stop after the push to the right. Remember dodging is 'still retaining possession of the ball'.

THE LEFT DODGE

In this dodge you do retain possession of the ball literally throughout. Again practice it in twos. Dribble up to your partner as before going straight for her stick and when you are within a couple of feet of it step to the left with your left foot, *pull* the ball towards you, immediately turn your stick to face forwards again and 'catch' the ball as you step forward with your right foot and carry on dribbling forwards. Your feet and the ball have, in fact, made two right-angled turns. The pull is just sufficient to carry the ball out of reach of your opponent's stick. It is important to remember that your feet remain on the *left* of the ball throughout. Now practise this with your partner moving forward to tackle and you will find that it is much easier to perform successfully. In fact, the faster she advances towards you the easier the dodge, hence the fact that forwards always love defence who rush towards them! Again the sight of her stick within inches of the ball is your signal to pull the ball away and the timing in this dodge is even more important than in the right dodge. You will discover the distance you pull

DIAGRAM I

DODGES

Right dodge

Left dodge

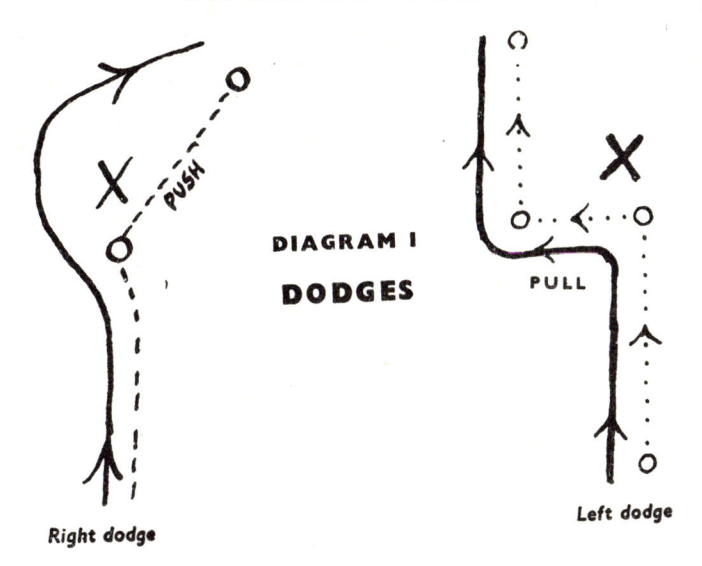

the ball away from her will vary according to her speed. I have done it successfully many times only moving the ball five or six inches.

THE LIFT OVER

This is nothing but a small controlled scoop stroke. As your opponent comes in to tackle keep your hands apart, lean forward, slant your stick, in order to get the blade under the ball and lift it over her stick, retrieving it the other side and continuing with your dribbling. The fact that the ball is lifted means that the dodge must be done with the utmost control. Hockey is meant to be played on the ground and any ball in the air must be put there with skill and understanding. It is obvious that the sooner you have your ball back on the end of your stick the better so there is no need to raise the ball to unnecessary heights. If you give little warning of your dodge your opponent's reaction will not be quick enough to enable her to lift her stick in time and therefore the height of the ball in theory need not be more than eight or nine inches. Usually, however, when this dodge is performed the ball is raised to a height of approximately a foot or eighteen inches. It should only be attempted on a good ground where one can rely on getting the blade under the ball at the right time. Make sure your ball is well over to your right as you approach the tackler so that you don't collide in the process!

Don't forget that in all dodging you, in possession of the ball, have the advantage. Any tackler can only react *after* you and you should make full use of the second's difference in time. That great asset of *acceleration* that I mentioned before is just the thing for this. Change the pace and the direction and hey presto! you are three-quarters on the way to success!

TACKLING

Dodging is the outcome of tackling. In the previous chapter we have assumed that the player is skilful enough in the art of dodging to avoid all tackles. If that were the case we should have a delightful scene of all players dodging merrily in and out and round every obstacle leaving a bewildered team behind them. This is far from the case! Neither would it be necessary to write anything about the skill of tackling.

However, there *is* a skill in tackling and the good defender will not rush in madly and hopefully but hover, poised and balanced, eyes watching the ball, like a cat watching a mouse, waiting for the moment either when the player temporarily loses control of the ball or makes a mistake with her pass or dodge. The mere fact that the tackler has hovered and is still there in front of them is often enough to put forwards off so that they mis-hit or play right into the tackler's hands. The tackler has made the player with the ball make the first move. If, however, the forward is quite unperturbed by these tactics and is getting dangerously near the circle edge then the tackler must choose her moment going for the ball with her stick down, deliberately and firmly with her hands apart giving her maximum control of her stick. Then having got the ball her one aim should be immediately to turn defence into attack.

DODGING AND TACKLING

Tackling, of course, is not always done by a defender to a forward or in a face to face position. Forwards can be a wonderful help to their own defence by tackling back and halves and backs that have been passed must always try to catch up and re-tackle. These are the occasions when a lunge tackle or a jab are most useful.

LUNGE TACKLE

Imagine a left wing dribbling the ball at full speed down the wing. Her opposing right half is running behind in an effort to catch her up but her speed is not enough to allow her to overtake and her last resort for any kind of a tackle must be by lunging forward with her left hand only on her stick in the hope that she can delay her wing sufficiently to enable her to get round her and face her for a full tackle. This is the left hand lunge tackle (Plate xiii). The player is on the right of the player with the ball running in the same direction and the fact that she has removed her right hand from her stick enables her to reach out even further. Her weight is forward on her front foot as she lunges swinging her stick round in a sweeping movement to finish with the blade against the ball. This is only *half the tackle*. Her immediate next move must be to move her feet round and position herself facing the left wing at the same time replacing her right hand on her stick from which position she can complete the tackle. Throughout the whole tackle she must play the ball only—if there is any interference of the forward's stick, feet, legs or body then she has obstructed and quite rightly the umpire should blow the whistle for an infringement of the obstruction rule. This is all done on the move, of course, and therefore needs considerable skill to perform successfully.

THE JAB TACKLE

This is also an emergency stroke and can be made from either side of a player with either hand on the stick.

Again let us imagine this time a right wing dribbling the ball down the pitch and her opposing left half not sufficiently in front of her to make a full tackle but running along side her on her left. The half's tactics are again delaying tactics. With one hand on her stick only, to allow her to reach out, she jabs at the ball as the wing taps it forward (Plate xii). Having once knocked it off its original pathway, again she must use all her powers of footwork to get round to face the right wing in order to complete the tackle. If she fails to do this and succeeds only in jabbing the ball off the side line at least she has temporarily stopped the attack.

If the play is over on the other side of the pitch and the left wing is again in possession of the ball the right half in using this tackle may have her right hand only on her stick. There is perhaps certainly less chance of her obstructing like that but many people will argue that presumably her right hand will be at the top of the handle if she is to get maximum reach and will therefore be in the wrong position when the left hand is returned —it is merely a matter of opinion.

In all tackling remember you play the ball—not the player, not her feet, nor her stick but the ball. And remember too, in big capital letters CONFIDENCE. You can apply that word to practically everything you do in hockey. Don't let the fact, that the approaching player in possession of the ball has already applied the same attitude, put you off. Someone has got to win, that's what the game is all about.

CHAPTER VI

TEAM TACTICS—CORNERS

A TEAM may have eleven capable individuals but they will never be successful unless they understand each other's aims and think of themselves as a team—a unit with each member a vital part. You, in your own position, have got your own job to do but it is very important that you realize what the responsibilities of the other members of your team are as well as your own. You can then fit in with the general plan instead of remaining in isolated ignorance. Let's take a general view of the team before the bully-off of the game.

Usually there are five forwards standing along the centre line one of whom, the centre forward, is ready to bully. Further back behind the line will be the three half backs. Behind them will be two full backs, one standing nearer the line than the other, and finally, a solitary figure, the goalkeeper, on guard at the goalmouth.

Their jobs? First the forwards—simply and purely to shoot goals. Although don't feel that if you are playing a back or a half it isn't your job to shoot goals too. It doesn't matter who goes up to score as long as there is understanding amongst the team. Similarly the forwards may well find themselves needed in defence, but the general idea is that the forwards shoot the goals and it is this line of five who make up the attack. The half backs, as their name suggests, are not solely defenders, but part of their time is spent in attacking as well so they are in fact half-forwards. They defend when their goal is being attacked, they attack when their forwards are attacking by backing them up and giving them all the support they need. They must therefore be most energetic, versatile and conscientious people. The job of the two backs, by guarding the

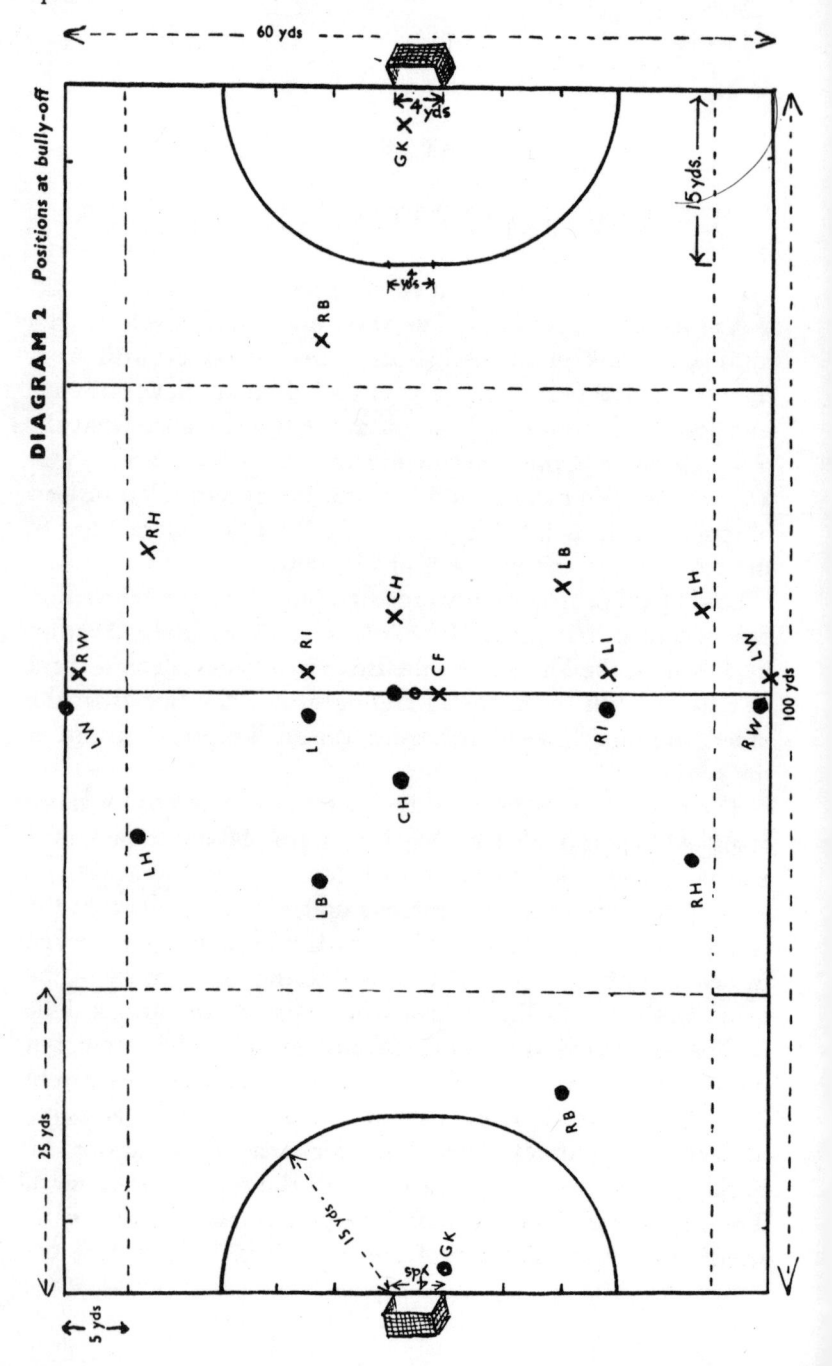

DIAGRAM 2 *Positions at bully-off*

approach to the goal behind them, is to break up all attacks made on that goal. You will notice that, in the diagram showing positions at bully-off, the left back is standing very much nearer to the centre line than the right back is. This is because there is an unwritten rule that the two backs never stand level with each other, but when one is forward the other is further back. We will discuss this later. Lastly, the goalkeeper's responsibility is to prevent at all costs the ball crossing that line in front of her goal.

Now it is easy to see that the team splits itself into two groups, one of attackers and one of defenders, but it is necessary to point out that these are general divisions. Backs who are only on the defensive and cannot start an attacking movement have not really completed their job. Similarly, forwards who are not prepared to tackle back or come back and help their defence when needed are not playing their full part. The attacking spirit must be apparent throughout the team—a goal may be 'made' as far back as a kicking clearance by the goal-keeper, helped on its way by backs and half backs and after co-operation with other forwards finally shot into the net by the right inner. She is the scorer but the team have all played their part. If each member of the team does her own job to the best of her ability, is sympathetic and understanding towards her colleagues and sets out to enjoy the game, then that team will have that valuable and beneficial quality that we call 'team spirit'.

There are certain situations in the game which are included in this chapter because they are not individual responsibilities but involve two or more players.

CORNERS

A corner is awarded when the ball has crossed over the goal line (other than in the goal mouth) after having been touched or sent off by a defender. There are two kinds of corners, long and short which is the penalty corner, and the umpire should state which has been awarded. Whichever the case it is a disadvantage to the defending team and an advantage for the

42

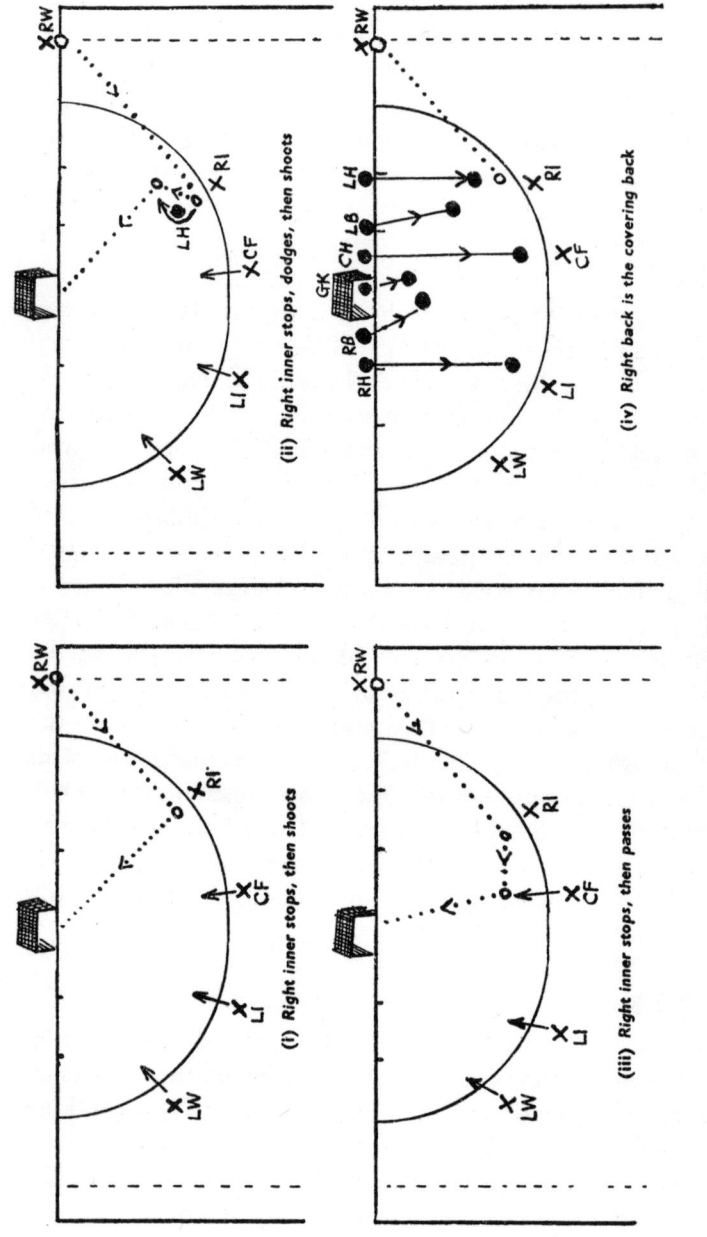

(i) Right inner stops, then shoots

(ii) Right inner stops, dodges, then shoots

(iii) Right inner stops, then passes

(iv) Right back is the covering back

DIAGRAM 3

CORNERS

attacking team; that sounds an obvious statement but it is as well to note it. The defending players of the one team and the forwards of the other, therefore, are the players directly involved. Have a look at their positions now at the corner before the hit is taken. All the defence will have their feet and sticks behind the goal line. The goalkeeper will be in the goal, the right back and right half on the right of the goal, the left back and left half on the left and the centre half standing near to one of the goal posts according to the side from which the ball is coming. Or some goalkeepers may like to have one of the backs in the goal-mouth with her to remain there as a sort of last line of defence to pick up anything that may get past her. Various teams have varying defensive tactics at corners and it is a good idea to experiment, bearing in mind the players you have got in your team. Some players, for example, may be very quick off the mark and prefer to get out to the forwards, someone else may have a very good eye for the ball and feel confident enough to stay on the line. There will be another player on this line—the wing taking the corner hit who must have the ball on the line at a spot nor more than five yards from the corner flag at a long corner, or ten yards from the goal post at a short corner. Her colleagues, the remaining four forwards, will be standing round the edge of the circle and must have their feet and sticks outside it. Their united aim is a goal as quickly and as neatly as possible and let me repeat here that a corner is an advantage to the attacking team—goals should and must result.

The aim of the defending players is first to prevent one and secondly to turn defence into attack as soon as possible.

Imagine you are the right wing taking a long corner. You collect the ball quickly, put it in position, decide upon the exact spot you are aiming for and get ready so that the moment that all defending players are behind the line you can hit the ball. It is a long corner, so you will probably hit the ball either to the right inner or the centre forward. To hit it further across to the left inner might be dangerous unless you have a particularly strong drive and can be quite sure that you can get the ball to her in good time.

Suppose you decide upon the right inner. She will want the ball to arrive in the circle just in front of her, so that all she has to do is to stop it and shoot. If your hit is inaccurate she will have to spend time re-positioning herself before shooting and a goal may be missed. So look at your target, make a mental note of her position in relation to your own, look down at the ball again and hit it hard so that it travels smoothly, quickly and accurately. Try to get as little back swing to your stroke as possible so that the defending players have only a short warning of the actual hit. After you have hit the ball, run forwards immediately and get on-side. It is very easy to stand and stare, in a somewhat detached attitude, leaving the rest of your forwards to finish off the attack, but they may need you and in any case you may be caught off-side unless there are three defenders between you and the goal.

The forward receiving the ball, in this case the right inner, can do one of three things: (*a*) shoot immediately, (*b*) dodge and then shoot, (*c*) pass. If she has got time she will stop the ball and shoot immediately aiming, not for the goalkeeper but to one or the other side of her. She will follow up her shot in case the goalkeeper gets her foot to it and so too will the left inner and centre forward. If she finds a defending player uncomfortably near and has not got time to shoot she must first dodge. Probably the best thing to do in this case is to stop the ball, push it to the right, out of line with the oncoming defending player and then having got behind her shoot, again following up the shot. She can, of course, use any of the dodges we have already discussed if there is sufficient space.

Her third alternative is to control the ball and then pass it to another player for her to shoot. She may need to do this if the ball is travelling very slowly towards her; she must run to meet it, control it and then pass it straight across the circle. Or she may deliberately pretend to be taking the shot herself and at the last minute try and find fault in the defence by passing it to her centre forward. As a third alternative, you, as the right wing have positioned yourself at her side to receive a little push pass and take a flying shot.

These tactics can be adapted and used by any of the forwards receiving the ball from either side. For example, a left inner receiving the ball from the left wing may shoot immediately, or she may do a left hand dodge round an opponent and then shoot or even push pass the ball to her right for her centre forward or right inner to use.

You can see then that there are a number of different tactics available to the forwards at a corner and the more they vary them and use them intelligently the better results they will have. You may like to try and think up more, for example, stopping the ball with your hand instead of your stick.

Remember too that at a long corner the ball may also be hit from a point on the *side* line within five yards of the corner flag and that at a short corner you have the choice of using either side for the hit. We nearly always make the wings take the corner hit but there is no rule about this and an enterprising captain will try out alternatives if necessary to obtain improvement. At your next team practice experiment a little. Here is an opportunity for the unexpected that may be just enough to upset your opponents and while they are getting over the shock allow you to crack in a goal. Psychological warfare! In any case I do think it is a good idea at your team practices to come to some conclusion about your corners so that you will all know what is going on.

We have dwelt a long time on the forwards. Let's make sure, as defending players now, that we know exactly what we are doing at a corner. The aim of all of them, as I have said is to prevent a goal being scored and to get the ball to their own forwards as quickly as possible.

As our example we will imagine the opposing left wing is taking a long corner. The first thing to do, and this will have been done long before the game started I hope, is to decide which out of the right back and the right half is going out first to that dangerous left inner standing in front of them. There is nothing in the rules to help them—they must decide for themselves. Usually it is the half-back who does the job. She, then, will sprint, yes sprint, with her stick down, as fast as she can, the moment the corner hit takes place to the stick of that left inner. She will have positioned herself beforehand opposite the stick side of the inner so that she runs the shortest distance—in a straight line. The right back will know all this and will follow up behind her half back in case she is eluded or fails to get to the inner in time in which case the shot must be intercepted by her.

Moving along the line we come to the centre half whose job is comparatively uncomplicated since she only ever has to be concerned with the opposing centre forward and she will therefore get out to her as quickly as possible and mark her as closely as possible.

Now what about the remaining left back and left half? First of all the left back. She becomes now what we call the 'covering' back. That is, she leaves her particular opponent the right inner in the capable hands of her own left half and she positions herself behind her fellow back ready to intercept a shot from the left. In doing this she must be most careful not to unsight her goalkeeper and it is up to the goalkeeper to inform her politely if she does. It is very easy to unsight your own goalkeeper and it is a thing that you must be constantly aware of. You cannot expect her either to enjoy the view of your back or save a goal if she cannot follow the game.

The left half, as I have said, has moved in to mark the right inner. This leaves the opposing right wing unmarked but we can safely allow this because it is unlikely that she can be of any immediate danger as she is the player farthest away from the ball. If, however, she is used, the defence must be ready in a second to switch their positions. It is most important that they work like clockwork, as you can see, but sometimes a spring breaks or a cog wheel gets displaced and a goal is scored. That's how the game is won or lost.

CHAPTER VII

TEAM TACTICS—FREE HITS

THE extraordinary thing about free hits is that they are so often wasted. It is not an uncommon sight to see the player taking the free hit take up her position, look around the field as the batsman does before the bowler's delivery on the cricket field, make quite sure everyone, friends and foes alike, are ready and proceed to hit the ball straight to an opposing player in front of her who if she has any initiative at all will immediately start an attack whilst everyone else is anticipating play to move in the other direction. Now it is not always the fault of the hitter of the ball—let us not paint her quite so black; but in my opinion it is extremely important to take free hits as quickly as possible. They are after all, an advantage to your side, a penalty against the other team for some infringement of a rule, and to make the most of that advantage the speed with which they are taken is certainly important.

You may say at this point that it is stupid to take a free hit so quickly that your own forwards do not have time to get ready but my answer is that as forwards they must always be ready, always anticipating and their defence must expect them and train them to be so. If they presume to play the game they must also learn the rules and if they know the rules they will, more often than not, know what the foul was and to which side the free hit has been awarded. Immediately, therefore, that they hear the whistle, if they are alive to the situation as they should be, they will realize what is going on, check their decision with a hurried glance at the umpire (it always helps to know where the umpire is I find!) and act accordingly. There should then be hardly a stoppage in the game except momentarily when the ball must be stationary before the hit is made and if defence and forwards alike understand this, I am sure there will be better results. There are, of course, the occasions when it is not possible to take the free hit so quickly, either because the ball has first had to be retrieved or the person taking the free hit has not been on the spot. In mentioning the latter point I would say that it does not always have to be a defence player to take the hit and if a forward is suitably placed she should take it without hesitation.

Whoever it is, the player has a choice of two alternatives: she can hit the ball to a player and by that I mean directly on to her stick or she can hit the ball into a space created by that player who will run into the space to collect the ball. She must make up her own mind quite clearly which she is doing and do it quickly and accurately. The type of stroke she uses will depend largely on how far she wants the ball to go. It is, of course, quite possible to drive the ball a short distance but I think in this case it is much easier to get a 'sympathetic' pass by using the push stroke. You will see that page 16 of the Rules Book states that 'the ball shall be stationary and shall be hit along the ground or pushed along the ground'.

To return to those two alternatives, if a player is marked closely it is obviously not wise to send the ball to her directly. She will realize this and so move to one side or the other to make a space, hence the second alternative, into which the ball can be sent. She may have deliberately drawn her marker away from the spot and leave the ball to be collected by a colleague.

There is, you see, and must be, complete understanding. It's a team tactic, a combined effort, not just a blind hit in the hope that the ball may get to someone on your side. That is not hockey. On the other hand if she wants the ball directly to her, she must show exactly where she wants it by placing her stick and turning the blade to the ball to receive it. This is most important—how often do we see forwards dancing around in front of their defence oblivious of the fact that they are being of no help whatsoever because they have not shown where they

PLATE I. The grip for dribbling. Note that the back of the left wrist is facing forwards, index fingers are spread comfortably.

DRIBBLING

PLATE II. Dribbling—front view. The back of the left wrist is leading the way: ball slightly to the right, stick close to ball.

PLATE III. Dribbling—side view. Plenty of space between hands and body. Keep the ball ahead of you all the time.

PLATE IV. The grip for driving. Hands together at the top of the stick; fingers curled round handle, inverted 'V's' in line with each other.

PLATE V. The drive. Head over the ball, weight on right foot, back lift need not be too high—timing is what matters.

THE DRIVE

PLATE VI. The point of contact. Weight transferred to left foot.

PLATE VII. The follow-through. Arms and stick in straight line pointing after the ball.

PLATE VIII. Hands apart; step up to the ball with left foot; get the weight BE-HIND the stroke.

PLATE IX. *Place* stick to ball

THE PUSH-SCOOP STROKE

PLATE X. A strong, powerful stroke ending in a follow-through that is low and forwards—stick pointing after ball.

PLATE XI. One hand only on stick for further reach; a delaying tactic only.

THE JAB TACKLE

PLATE XII. Follow-up of the jab tackle. Both hands on stick, run feet round to face opponent. Note the space between the players' bodies to avoid obstruction.

PLATE XIII. Again a one-handed delaying action followed up by . . .

THE LUNGE TACKLE

PAGE XIV. A two-handed tackle facing opponent.

want the ball. You cannot expect your defence to read your mind as well as concentrate on everything else. Ask for the ball, and if you haven't and it comes in the wrong place you have only yourself to blame. If you have and done your best to make it clear where you want it then you have played your part at a free hit. One last reminder—you must be at least five yards away from the person taking the hit.

THE HIT-OUT

When the ball goes out of play over the goal line from an attacker, the game is re-started by a hit out taken opposite the spot where it crossed the goal line and 15 yards from it, that is level with the front of the shooting circle. During the season 1969–70, all pitches were marked with a 16-yard shooting circle, as in men's hockey, and the hit-out, therefore, was taken from a spot 16 yards and not 15 yards from the goal line. This is only an experiment at the moment which may or may not be adopted into the rules at a later date. Similarly, the use of allowing a substitute when a player is injured is also to be experimented for a whole season and we shall have to wait and see whether or not this becomes a definite rule.

To return to our hit-outs. It is very necessary to have some sort of plan in mind at a hit-out, so often they are completely wasted like the ordinary free hits that take place during the game, and so often, as before, it isn't always the fault of the hitter. As in the previous paragraphs about free hits other players *must* help. Being such a defensive free hit it is, of course, even more important that the ball is not immediately intercepted by the opposition who would then be in a very attacking position.

Firstly, as in ordinary free hits anywhere on the field, if you see a member of your team free and ready to receive the ball, then use her quickly and accurately. Alternatively, if there is a space large enough for you to get the ball through with a good drive for one of your team to run on to, that is just as good.

However, often neither of these possibilities are there,

D

especially if you have taken a long time to retrieve the ball and all the opposition have been able to position themselves marking both players and spaces. You must now in this situation, try to draw them out of position by short passing before the final pass through is made. Remember with all free hits, it isn't always necessary to pass from defence to forward straight away, and it isn't always necessary to make the first pass an attacking one. Practise, if you are a right back, for instance, taking a hit-out, passing the ball with a push stroke to your right half who is standing 7 or 8 yards away, level with you. She may then see a gap, because one of the opposition has moved, into which to send her attacking pass; or she may return the ball to you again to wrong foot an opponent. You can gain ground as you do this passing and as long as you both understand what is happening and are careful and on the look out for any possible interception you should find a way through ultimately.

A second tactic at hit-outs is to use the wing. She stands further up the field, probably marked, until the ball is ready to be hit and then runs back straight down the side line to receive a very square hit from the back. If she is a right wing she must be ready to run her feet round quickly in order to get control of the ball, and if she is a left wing to perhaps pull the ball sharply towards her out of range of an opponent's stick. Of course this needs practice because it needs correct timing above all and complete understanding.

Finally to sum up about free hits wherever they are taken. Think of it this way. You are the team with the advantage. To waste that advantage is a waste of energy and time—you might as well have let the other side have the ball in the first place. ·Free hits may be taken by anyone to anyone. They may be hit forwards, sideways or backwards. Be free and easy, about them, not nonchalant, but enterprising and enjoy them.

CHAPTER VIII

TEAM TACTICS—ROLLS-ON

SIMILARLY these too call for understanding and combined effort if they are to be put to the fullest use. Here again we all too frequently see a roll-on that eventually peters out until in no time at all the other team are in possession of the ball and have already turned defence into attack. You must make the fullest use of your roll—take the advantage that the umpire has given you quickly and intelligently. It is obviously something that must be practised and worked out at your team practices.

I suggest that you try these four alternatives if you are rolling the ball on in your game.

(*a*) Roll it to your wing
(*b*) Roll it to your inner
(*c*) Roll it to your back
(*d*) Roll it to your centre forward

Let's deal with them one by one. Firstly, to the wing. This is the ball that you roll right up the side line, make no mistake about it, roll it as near and as parallel to the side line as you can. If you are right half use your left hand, if you are a left half use your right hand. But whichever you are, see that your feet and your stick, which you must have in your hand remember, are behind the line and get down to it. Get the back of your rolling hand almost brushing the grass as you roll the ball (Plate xiv). Look where you are going to send the ball and get your action as smooth as possible timing your swing so that the ball literally does roll out of the palm of your hand along the ground instead of hitting the turf and bouncing away. Then immediately straighten up, step back on to the pitch, put both hands on your stick and be ready to continue play. There's a tendency here to stand back and take a long distant view of the job you've done so be alert in case the ball comes your way more quickly than you expected.

Now about the one to the inner. There's a difference here which I will talk about to the inners themselves, but the inner will not be standing still—at least I hope she won't be. So often we see at rolls-on an agitated half back looking for somewhere to roll the ball and in front of her a neat row of players, amongst whom are her wing and inner and back—glued to the five yard line, all standing still, all being very nicely marked in the intervening spaces by the opposition. The situation is hopeless. So you must have an understanding with your inner that she does not stand on the five yard line but she suddenly appears and you roll the ball to her as she does so. It may sound a little magical I agree but believe me, because I do it as often as I can when I'm playing left inner, it pays dividends nearly every time. I should add, that you must have an understanding with your inner too that, able as she is in this appearing act, you will not always use her—you must keep the other side guessing, and the more you can do this in any game the more skilfully you are playing it.

The third alternative is to your own back. Only attempt this when you are far away enough from your own goal (let's say anywhere beyond the twenty-five yard line) for it to be safe, and only attempt it also when there is sufficient space between you and the back and the rest of the players further up the field. It is a surreptitious little roll from the palm of your hand which has started out to be a roll ahead of you but by turning your hand over and changing direction quickly it does in fact go behind you or to your side. Here it is even more important to recover your position on the field quickly as the back will probably receive the ball, control it and push it back to you for you to drive hard up the side line to your wing or push in to your inner. If the back does not use you, she will make the pass herself but in either case the ball, we hope, will have covered a considerable amount of ground in the right direction.

TEAM TACTICS—ROLLS-ON

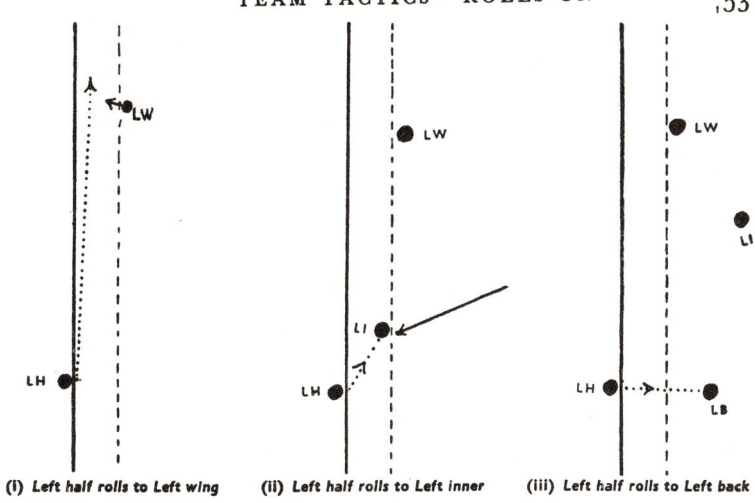

(i) Left half rolls to Left wing   (ii) Left half rolls to Left inner   (iii) Left half rolls to Left back

DIAGRAM 4

The fourth alternative, to be used occasionally if the conditions are favourable, is to roll the ball hard to your centre forward. The opposing centre half may be caught off guard not marking her closely enough and your centre forward may be free to receive a long roll from you.

So you see rolls-on involve a number of players—they are not only the responsibility of the half back. As with free hits you may use anyone, don't be too rigid about the four alternatives I have suggested. You may, for instance, have a player on your side of the field who likes you just to drop the ball near to the side line for her to collect quickly and unexpectedly, or you may happen to notice one of your team free whom you have never used before at a roll-on. Be aware of the possibilities—they are almost endless.

CHAPTER IX

GOALKEEPER

IN the following chapters we will study *your* particular position. All the things we have discussed so far have been either individual skills, like learning to dribble or to push the ball, or team tactics which have involved the understanding and co-operation of a number of players. Now we will go through the whole team and pick out the main essentials necessary for a player in each of the eleven positions.

All my hockey, as a forward, has been concerned with shooting at, or to be precise, around a goalkeeper. That's the way I like it but it means that at a time like this, I find it rather difficult to imagine myself as a goalkeeper—at the receiving end as it were. Certainly, on reflection, goalkeepers are to be admired. To stand between two posts armed with a thin hockey stick and protected only up to the knees, and face a number of people whose sole aim is to shoot at you seems to me to be exceedingly courageous. On the other hand I can easily see that the position of goalkeeper in the team offers an attraction of its own, which is unlike any of the other positions on the field and which is therefore bound to appeal to the kind of player who gets a thrill out of stopping a shot just as much as a forward gets in shooting one.

There are, however, certain qualities that she must possess that are common to all the players. We have already touched on some of them; she must be fit, very quick to react, have most agile feet, have also a sense of awareness perhaps even more so than the other members of her team, and possess that most useful asset—the ability to anticipate. She is, as we know, the only person in the team who is allowed to kick the ball and she must learn to control the ball with her foot just as the rest of us learn to with our sticks. In just the same way that we 'give' back with our stick as we field the ball, so she receives the ball on her pads or feet with knees slightly bent, in a supple, almost relaxed position, to prevent the ball from rebounding off her pads. Watch any good goalkeeper—she is never standing up stiffly but always bent a little, her weight forward, and following the game whether the ball is in her half of the field or not. She must keep her eye on the ball all the time, particularly closely, of course, when a shot at goal is forthcoming. This is where the anticipation will be used and she will then position herself accordingly.

If you are a goalkeeper always stand well in front of the line —it's not much good if it is a goal before it ever reaches you— and practise kicking the ball in every direction with both feet, until you are pretty sure that you can use them equally well. You will probably prefer to kick with one foot more than the other but it is important to practise with both because you have not always enough time to use your favourite foot nor indeed is it always wise to do so. Generally speaking if the ball is coming to your left you will clear to your left and if to your right you will clear to that side, but the main thing to bear in mind is that you clear into a space or to someone of your own side. So much can be done by you if you remember this and do not think of yourself as merely stopping the ball. That's only half your job, finish it off by sending your team away with an intelligent and accurate clearance and then you will have earned full marks as a goalkeeper.

You have the choice, as I said, of aiming that clearance either to a space or to one of your own team. The latter, I think, is preferable providing she is well positioned for it, for it is unwise to have a loose ball anywhere in the circle for long, but at all costs avoid sending the ball straight back to an opponent. If you are challenged by a forward always try and clear the ball to her non-stick side—she won't like that so much.

All these kicks, by the way, should be made with the inside of your foot, not the toe cap, and remember to lean forward as you kick. If your weight is back when you clear the ball it will probably go up in the air, you cannot direct it so accurately, and you will quite likely get stopped for dangerous kicking.

There is a rule, as you know I expect, that you must have your stick in your hand but when you first have a go at goalkeeping don't be tempted to use it—get your feet right first and then when you are sure of them and have confidence in them you can start to think about your stick. It is useful sometimes; have it in your right hand and use it for deflecting cross shots on your right if you cannot get your foot to the ball, or if you do not deflect the ball but stop it dead and have not time to get to it, put your left hand back on to your stick and push the ball clear along the goal line. Remember that corners are better than goals but do be careful not to give away unnecessary corners, that is why it is so important to get an accurate kick with your foot. Practise, aiming at a target and check up on your accuracy.

Shots will not always come to you along the ground and you must be prepared, of course, to stop anything anywhere from going between those posts behind you. These sort of shots you will stop with either your left hand or your pads according to their height and position. If you catch a ball high up above you, let it drop straight down immediately (it would be to your disadvantage in any case if it rebounded although you would not be penalized for this if the umpire considered it to be unintentional) and then clear as quickly as you can.

What about bullies? Although we allow you the privileges of kicking the ball and of a rebounding ball, or 'knocked on' ball, we don't allow any other infringements of the rules from you. If you do, and you stop a certain goal by doing so you're in for a penalty bully so be careful—perhaps it might be wise to practise bullying just in case and remember you lose your privilege of being able to kick the ball during a penalty bully.

CHAPTER X

BACKS

WHETHER you are a right or a left back you must work very much in league with each other, for only by so doing can you succeed in guarding the goal behind you. You must have complete understanding and co-operation from each other.

First of all there are all the numerous qualities necessary to the player of any position on the hockey field that we must consider before going on to the specific jobs of the right and left backs. Such things as anticipation, that is in other words understanding of the situation and a conclusion arrived at as to the best action to be taken—a wealth of value to any player. Then having decided upon the correct thing to do the speed and physical ability to perform it—quick mental and physical reaction after the anticipation. Intelligence therefore must play its part. Then confidence—without which nothing can be performed perfectly; the quality of being able to direct your physical actions from a fully co-operating brain. You are in no two minds about the matter. You have seen, considered, and acted. And then purely and simply the skill to do whatever you have decided to do—the control of the ball, your stick, your feet and body.

Our two backs need all these qualities; and they need also the special knowledge of the situations which will arise that are peculiar to their positions. They need to know about 'covering', marking, tackling and positioning; they need to know also exactly how and where they fit in as defence members in the complete picture of the team and how they must combine with the half backs to form that defence.

Easily the most important thing a back must get right is the tactic of 'covering'. It means placing oneself in such a position that you form a second line of defence after your other back has been defeated instead of having been passed simultaneously with her at an oncoming attack from your opponents. That is why we always make it an unwritten rule that you and your other back never stand opposite or 'square' with each other at any time. If you do, you are asking for disaster. It is obvious, if you think about it, that if two backs are standing level with each other facing an attacking forward in possession of the ball that if she passes one she passes both. The one thing that defence players must *never* allow is to let two defenders be beaten at the same time; it is inevitable that many times one will be passed, that is how teams win or lose matches.

We have established then that one defender at a time goes forward to meet the oncoming forward whilst her colleagues in the defence team lie in wait in case her mission is unsuccessful. Who goes and who waits depends on the place of the attack. Let us suppose the opposing right inner is in possession of the ball and is dribbling down the field. She is the particular responsibility of the left back who will therefore advance steadily towards her in order to check the attack. The right back will see this and understand it and will drop back towards her own goal ready to go across to her left if necessary to tackle the right inner if she has evaded the left back. The right back has then 'covered' her left back, that is she has positioned herself so as to provide a second line of defence to that attacking right inner. Likewise in a similar situation on the other side of the field the left back may 'cover' her right back. We will follow the same situation a little further to get a complete picture of this defence system and how the two backs must have co-operation from their wing halves.

That right inner is dribbling the ball, under complete control, and looking most dangerous, towards you—the left back. You are there to tackle or to make her pass. In either case you hope you will break up the attack. If you tackle, you choose your moment and with your stick down go in for the ball firmly and confidently and when you have got it you turn, as quickly and as beneficially as possible, defence into attack. Or secondly you make her pass. It may be a bad pass, too weak and made too soon, which you can intercept or it may be successful in reaching another attacker who is not your direct responsibility—in which case you have at least checked your opponent, the dangerous-looking right inner. Now suppose the pass is to the right wing. Your left half is looking after the right wing marking her closely or marking the space head of her. If, however, she is beaten, you must be prepared to take her place but at the same time keep an eye on your right inner who may be used again.

Let's suppose that opposing right wing has received her pass, dodged her left half and is dribbling the ball down the wing nearing the circle. As a left back you will not be tempted too soon to tackle her thus leaving your right inner unmarked neither will you leave it too late until the wing is in the circle and able to get in a shot at goal. You make your tackle just before she arrives at the circle edge and your right back will know this and will have come across to cover you and keep an eye on the right inner for you as well. This leaves the right back's particular opponent, the left inner, unmarked but as soon as the right back moves across, her right half will have noticed this and come in to take her place in marking the left inner. They have all then moved across one place and they mark their new opponents until the attack has been broken up. The only opposing attacker who is not marked is the left wing but as she is farthest away from the ball it is not likely that she can be of any real danger. Of course, if the ball is suddenly swung across to her side of the field the whole defence team must move back again to their original positions. They must be extremely mobile then—gone are the days when we think of a back as the most solid player on the field to be rebounded from. It is not unusual these days for a back to come up and receive a corner hit on the edge of the circle. Why shouldn't she if she has the best shot on the field? Now that right inner may alternatively pass to her left, either to her centre forward or to the left inner or left wing. The first pass will be dealt with by the centre half who is the only person in this system of defence play who never leaves her opponent—she sticks to her centre forward like glue and only by doing so can she be of any help to the rest of her defence colleagues.

The pass to the left inner will naturally involve the right back marking her. She will tackle, or better still intercept the pass before it ever reaches the left inner and her left back will cover and be ready to go across to her right if needed.

The other alternative pass from that right inner to her left wing means the right half will be called upon to be the first line of defence. The right back will be near at hand and the left back will have dropped back nearer her own goal, covering.

The two backs, then, work like a pulley. One is up the field and the other is further back nearer her own goal according to which side of the field the play is at that particular moment. They are ready at a moment's notice to reverse their positions should the ball be swung to the other side of the field. They are concentrating, anticipating, positioning and moving all the time, and they are working in complete harmony with each other and with their wing halves. They are a solid and active defence who are capable not only of breaking up attacks from the opposition but of creating new ones for their own team.

MARKING

So much for 'covering' which you, whether you are a right back or a left back, must understand and use. I've mentioned a great deal the word 'marking' and it might be just as well to get clear in our minds quite briefly and simply what we mean when we say a player is marking another player. It means preventing that player from taking part in the game. Well, quite obviously it isn't always successful and marking is a battle of wits and physical skill between the marker and the marked; one must lose and one must win, but nevertheless the aim of the marker is to mark her player out of the game. To all intents and purposes she is there to do her very best to see that the player whom she is marking does not get the ball and if she does, is not allowed to do anything dangerous with it.

There is only one way to mark a player and that is on the stick side of her and between her and the goal into which she is playing. Now by the stick side of her we mean in such a position that we are able to play the ball with our stick against her stick. If two players stand facing each other with their sticks out as for dribbling with the ball between their sticks, their sticks are opposite each other but their bodies are not. The right shoulder of one will be opposite the right shoulder of the other. So stand where you can play the ball, not the player.

Secondly, stand between her and the goal into which she is playing: no matter how near you are to your opponent you are not marking her unless you are in such a position as to provide an obstacle for her to avoid *en route* for her goal. Assuming that she is a normal forward and will travel forwards in a normal way when she receives the ball and assuming that you are a marker whose aim is to stop her advances, it is obvious that there is only one side of her for you to stand if you are to be at all successful.

A word here about the distance you are away from the player whom you are marking. Either you (*a*) mark the player or (*b*) mark the space between and ahead of the player. You must make up your mind which you are doing and do it clearly. If you are marking the player then mark her as close as you can get without 'personally handling her', so that the moment the ball arrives at her stick your stick is there also. If on the other hand, you are marking the space with the idea of intercepting the ball before it reaches your opponent then position yourself still between her and the goal but in line with what you anticipate will be the path of the ball.

There are one or two other points to remember in helping you to play right or left back. I'm speaking now as a forward who has, on occasion, found it most irritating when having done my best to show where I want the ball from my defence,

I have received a most inconsiderate drive which is neither where I wanted it nor how I wanted it. So please, if you are a back, take a look at your forward before you send the ball to her (and tell her afterwards if she isn't making it clear where she wants it!) and send it sympathetically, either to her stick or to the space she has made for it and not at thirty m.p.h. if she is within a few yards of you. It's one of those things that is neither right nor wrong but does so much to cultivate a smooth-running and efficient team which is after all what we are aiming at. Then, secondly don't trust to luck and hit it as hard as you can hoping it will blast its way through the opposition and eventually reach your forward. There's no luck about defence play; there's no luck about hockey at all, or shouldn't be.

We have already dealt with tackling in Chapter 5 but just a reminder here that you haven't finished when your tackle has failed; get back as quickly as you can, you are always needed when an attack is on.

At corners too, you have a great responsibility; those forwards will be doing their utmost to convert the corner into a goal and your covering and marking must be as effective as you can possibly make it. Marking in this case will be the close kind—the closer the better and your clearances must be well positioned and never across the circle where opposing forwards can intercept and shoot. All the time, too, try and be aware of where you are in relation to your goalkeeper so that you never unsight her.

Don't imagine that dodging is solely a forward's job. The dodges we discussed in Chapter 5 can and must necessarily all be used by you as backs, the only difference being that you will probably be performing them in a rather more static position than the forward. Supposing an attacking forward in front of you has just received a pass, has not got complete control of the ball and lets it go too far forward on to your stick. You field the ball and as the onrushing forward tackles, you perform your dodge: pull the ball to your left, just out of reach of her stick, or if that will lead you into more trouble or

BACKS

too near to other forwards use the right dodge and push it to your right ahead of you just before her stick reaches the ball.

Alternatively use the flick over her stick which will be comparatively easy since you are standing still. Try these out with a partner. Get her to hit the ball to you and then immediately to rush towards you. Field it, keep your eyes on the ball and wait until you see her stick out of the corner of your eye and then dodge. It is a most satisfying experience, all a question of timing, and guaranteed to work if your forward is really rushing you. I have seen a back perform successive dodges with complete calm and perfect control and it is always a delight to see her emerge from a scene of confusion and flurried looking forwards behind her with the ball at her stick, her body poised and followed by a perfect attacking pass. That must be very satisfying to her too.

CHAPTER XI

RIGHT HALF

We will assume, although it is not a waste of time to repeat them, that our half backs have all the essential qualities that go to make up a good player: speed, stickwork, anticipation, concentration and determination and intelligence.

Of these the one most put to use perhaps, in the half back's case is anticipation (which is after all intelligence) for even though she has a specific job to do, and a very definite, and important one, there are a number of times when, unless she has learnt her job completely and understands it fully, she will be caught in the wrong place at the wrong time. That sounds a little complicated for our poor half back; so it is, but once she has mastered it and understands how and where she fits in with the whole defence unit, the acquired skill only makes her job the more enjoyable.

We will look at this problem from the right half's point of view only. First and foremost she is a defence player, but like any other defence player that is no reason to suppose that she is incapable of being, or disallowed to be, an attacking player also; I will talk of this later. Her job, then, as one of the defence team is to mark the opposing left wing. That is the player who is her particular responsibility and as a right half her prime aim is to see that that left wing does not receive the ball, and if she does, to do something about it quickly. This means marking and here we must refer to the previous chapter. It is sufficient at this point to repeat that marking a player means preventing that player from taking part in a movement by positioning oneself so that, ideally, she never gets the ball, or, as a second best that you are able to rob her of it immediately she does receive it. Now all these passes that an opposing left wing will be getting will be coming from her right or occasionally from directly behind her—she will never, unless she has interchanged with her left inner, receive a ball on her left. This at least helps the right half. Her area for marking lies always on the stick side of her opposing left wing. Let's suppose there is an attack on your side of the field. Unless you as a right half know that you can run faster than your left wing it is a risk to take to ever let her get a chance of a start on you, so generally speaking it is safer, I think, to mark that space ahead of your wing so that you can prevent any 'through' pass that is sent to her. If you are not quick enough and fail to intercept this pass then you have just got to turn round as quickly as you can and chase her —the fact that you are chasing her may well worry her and cause her to mis-hit or give a bad pass, but in any case you have made her pass the ball and you hope that your right back will be ready to deal with the pass. So don't feel that you've lost if you are passed or if you make a mistake—recover quickly and get back into the game.

If the attack is being made on the other side of the field, perhaps from the right inner, now is the time for you to put to use all you know about 'covering'. You will, I hope, have discussed this with the other members of the defence team, particularly your right back, and have got it quite clear that if she has been called away to defend or to cover the left back then you must take her place in marking the opposing left inner in the circle to prevent her from shooting. So you move across, not just a little way, that is neither here nor there, but you move so that you are close to her and are between her and where you think the ball will come from—always, of course, aware of your left wing whom you have left temporarily unmarked and always ready to switch back to your original task if the right back returns or the attack is moved to your side of the field and the left wing is used.

Supposing the attack is again on the far side of the field but has not yet developed and reached the defending '25' then your covering this time must be really deep. As before you will move across, because your left back will be up the field and the right back will be covering her and you in turn will cover the right back but very deeply and again according to the positions of the rest of your defence. As a defender then, you must be constantly watching, positioning and spoiling.

Before we go on to the attacking part of a right half's game let us for a moment consider her part at a defending corner. Again she will have a previous arrangement with her right back as to the tactics. If the corner is on her side, that is, being taken by the opposing left wing, it is usually her responsibility to mark the left inner and with that in mind she will place herself opposite that left inner slightly to the stick side of her where she imagines she will receive the ball and get out to her as quickly as possible when the corner hit is taken. Her right back will back up behind her. There is no need for this tactic to be used if the opposite alternative is preferred by both back and half; try it out for yourself and vary it if you like according to your opponents but always be quite clear what is expected of you and then do it to your utmost ability. The most important part of any of the defence players is to understand how and where they fit in the complete defence unit—the team that moves and plays as a whole and not as five individuals. So having shot like a bullet from that goal line as soon as the hit is taken, your aim is to get to the ball first or, as a next best, to tackle and block that left inner's shot. Having got the ball, clear it, never taking or passing it in this area but always out away from the goal and clear it intelligently with the dual aim of not only cancelling out an opponent's attack but of starting one in your own team as well. Now supposing the ball is not hit to the left inner; your tactics remain the same—you are there, marking as closely as you can, remember, because only close marking can be of any use in the defending circle and always ready to intercept if the ball should come your way.

If the corner hit is being taken on the far side from you, you will still mark the left inner if your right back is covering leaving the left wing temporarily unmarked.

Now for attacking play: remember half backs are not only half backs and that the other half is a half forward. This means that you mustn't hesitate if the chance lies ahead for you to shoot a goal. Don't think that you are not allowed to, or that you shouldn't or that the others might not like it if you do—whilst you are thinking all that you have lost the chance and the ball. Get it clear now—shoot if you have a chance. This doesn't mean that you go up on the forward line and forget all about looking after the opposing left wing if the opponents get the ball out to her, but I do like to see an attacking half back and any player, for that matter, who uses opportunities, conventional or otherwise. But attacking, of course, isn't just the shooting of goals and by far the most important role of the right half as an attacking half will be to see that she gives her own right wing and right inner plenty of work to do in the game. They are the players immediately in front of her, they are the players whom she will most frequently 'feed'. 'Feeding' is not pandering to them, they'll thank you for it, believe me, and instead of using energy in order to receive the ball in the first place they can use that energy to do something really constructive with it afterwards. So send your right wing and right inner off on to a good start—put the ball just where they want it and at the right speed.

Your passes, of course, are not always to those two players; a well-timed hard drive diagonally right across the field to your left inner or even your left wing will open out the game, delight your left inner who is moaning because the game is always on the other side, and cause the defence to switch their positions if they are to stop the attack. Remember this at free hits too if you see the chance. Free hits are given to you as compensation for an infringement of the rules—see to it that you take full advantage of that and use them intelligently. Make use of the back pass if necessary, don't feel that you've always got to send the ball forwards all the time.

Again, at rolls-on, if you are rolling the ball it is a complete waste of your time and energy if it is going to an opponent, you might as well have let them roll it on for you. It is up to you to see that you use the advantage given to you.

We have dealt in Chapter 8 with the various rolls-on that you can practise—try them all and vary them throughout the game, and practise using your left hand to roll. If your opponent is rolling the ball have an arrangement with your right back and right wing and right inner as to who is to mark who, but be prepared to waive this if your forwards are not back in time—it is not often that everything goes quite smoothly according to plan and it is all very well to play the game on paper, but it can never be the same as the real thing and it is only then that the individual must show her personal initiative. I think it is a good plan for your wing to take the rolls-on when it is in the attacking '25'; she is only in the way if she is on the five-yard line and it means that you are already in position for attack or defence. Be ready, however, in case she uses you.

Let's sum up this never-ending always positioning role of right half. She defends by marking the opposing left wing or the opposing left inner; by covering (deeply when play is on the far side of the field); by tackling anybody if she is the last line of defence. She attacks by backing up her right wing and right inner when they are attacking; by using free hits and rolls-on constructively; by having a shot at goal if the occasion arises. She plays the game by using her stick, her feet and her intelligence to the best of her ability at all times. Good luck to you right halves and keep fit for you very rarely get a rest!

CHAPTER XII

CENTRE HALF

LIKE the right half the centre half is just as much an attacking player as a defending one—perhaps even more so. In defence her most important job, of course—indeed her only job—is to mark the opposing centre forward. In attack her greatest help is in distributing the ball intelligently and in a way almost directing the flow of the game by giving passes to either side and to any of her forwards in front of her. It is obvious therefore that she must have the full range of all the strokes and be able to use them in any direction.

Let's deal with her job as a defender first of all. You as a centre half are solely responsible for that opposing centre forward and unlike any of the other defence players no-one will take your place should she pass you. You must realize how vital it is then that she does not pass you and this will give you plenty to get on with during the game. You are the pivot, we might say, around which the whole defence system of marking and covering revolves. You never have to cover or mark anyone else, unless there has been some interchanging of forwards, and you never, or very rarely, have to tackle anyone else. Your defence expect this of you and will only find you a nuisance and in the way if you do not practise it, for they can only get on with their plans of defence tactics if they can rely on the opposing centre forward always being taken care of by you. That's your job then as a defence player, that is how and where you fit in to the defence system. If that centre forward does get past, you have just got to turn and chase her for no-one else is going to do it for you. Practise until you improve and then go on improving by running and turning, backwards and forwards along the same line, keeping your stick down and doing it at full speed.

Your marking of your centre forward will vary according to where play is at the moment. If you are in mid-field or your team is attacking up near the opponent's goal then you are in front of your centre forward—between her and the ball, but not on the goal side of her, notice, as is usual in marking. In this position you are able to mark her by intercepting the ball if it is sent to her and at the same time you are able to back up your forwards in their attack. Your position when you are defending in the circle will be very much closer to the centre forward, as close as you can get, in fact, and on the goal side of her now so that you do not allow her to get her stick to the ball and shoot. Two positions then for marking both with the same aim—to mark the opposing centre forward out of the game. In the first you will need to use all the power of anticipation you possess; know where your centre forward is all the time even though she is behind you, be aware of her, make her feel by the time she comes off the field that you are tied to her by an invisible piece of string, and then by anticipation and positioning you are able to cut off all passes to her.

In marking her in the circle, stick to her like glue, demoralize her by never allowing her to get in a shot at goal, make it so difficult for her that she spends all her time trying to get rid of you instead of attacking and worry her. At a defending corner get out to her as quickly as you can with your stick down aiming for where you think she will receive the ball. Be ready for her to dodge and be ready also for the opposing centre half to have a go at shooting. It is not a good policy to tackle the opposing centre half in mid-field normally but this is an occasion when you must. So much for defence, except to say that with good footwork and anticipation you can do a tremendous amount of good by intercepting cross passes from your opponents in the middle of the field and breaking up an attack before it ever gets going. You can instil great confidence into your team, if you are the sort of centre half who is not only forever spoiling but following that up with determined constructive attacking passing, instead of the sort of centre half who is scurrying backwards and forwards as the ball is passed from inner to inner and never really seems to be doing much.

Centre half is a wonderful position to captain a team from—you are in such a commanding position.

Now for attacking. As we have already said you may shoot goals and if the opportunity arises waste no time in doing so, but if your forwards are in front of you pass the ball to them—it is their job remember! By far the greatest part of your attacking game is by backing up your forwards at their attacks —let them know that you are there just in case your opponents intercept, give them confidence and encouragement, be alert and ready to start and restart attacks, and don't ever let there be a large gap between you and them, a sort of no-man's land where you become detached and distant.

Good attacks are started by good passes. Choose the forward you think in the best position to receive the ball and try to put it exactly where she needs it. Notice quickly the positions of the opposing players near her; if there is room pass the ball into the space ahead of her or to one side of her for her to run on to, or if the space ahead is marked send the ball accurately to her stick. Alternatively she may have deliberately moved to one side, drawing her opponent with her, meaning you to use the space she has just made. So at all times try to understand your forwards' aims and wishes and give them accurate and sympathetic passes. Vary your passes, sometimes long drives, sometimes shorter pushes and use your power to open up the game by passing to the right and left. As in all games don't use the same pass too often, it makes it so much easier for your opponents to position themselves in readiness, and remember sometimes to use a good hard pass to the wings behind the rest of the forwards. This is particularly useful on the edge of the attacking circle when the opposing defence are busy concentrating on marking the inside forwards. So too, be ready yourself, if your wing has dribbled the ball too near to the goal line, to receive a back pass from her for you to shoot. At attacking corners take every opportunity to shoot. You may have a previous arrangement to receive the corner hit yourself or for your centre forward to stop it for you to shoot, but try out your own ideas when you are practising corners. Free hits must be taken quickly and intelligently and always be ready for that long roll-on from your wing half if she needs you.

Finally, commanding position you may have, but don't wander all over the field trying to do everyone else's work.

You've got an important job, yes; you need great stamina, yes; you are the pivot of the defence system, the director of the attacks, the distributor of the ball, true enough—but unless you stay in the centre of the field you may as well go and have tea.

CHAPTER XIII

LEFT HALF

I suppose one might say that the job of all those who play a defending game, those players whose aim is to spoil rather than attack, whether they be backs or half backs, is a three-fold one: they mark so that their opponent will not be used; they intercept if their opponent is used; they tackle if their opponent has been used; marking, intercepting, tackling—or, if you like, intelligence, anticipation and stickwork. These then are the essential qualities, as I have said many times before.

Marking—you as a left half will spend most of your time marking the opposing right wing. When she is attacking and in or near your defending circle you will be very close to her so that should she be used you can get your stick to the ball first. The passes that she is going to receive in such circumstances will be straight to her stick, and you mark not the space, not her back, but her stick—you position yourself all the time so that you are between her and the ball and your stick is very close to her stick.

In mid-field your marking will not be so close—if it is the right inner has only to send a 'through' pass ahead of the right wing and whilst you are turning round the speedy wing has run on to the ball and passed you. You must always be aware of that space, therefore, ahead of the right wing in mid-field. Remember it is easier to run forward, if you are alert and ready, and intercept, than it is to turn round and chase. The temptation is to come in too much, leaving too much space on your left, your difficult non-stick side, into which the ball can be sent. Keep out near the side line if you wish to avoid getting yourself into difficulties and practise your reversed stick fielding just in case. This positioning too near to the inner in mid-field play might lead you to think that you can tackle her but she, if she has any sense at all, will immediately notice this and send the ball to your unmarked right wing. You have done, in fact, exactly what she would have liked you to do, she may even have done her best to draw you to her, making it appear as if you have every chance of winning the tackle—you've no idea how wily these inners can be! So don't be tempted, stick to your right wing and make that inner think of something else.

There is the occasion, of course, when it is absolutely essential that you do mark that right inner and if you have read the previous chapters and understood about covering and marking in the defence system you will know that this is when there is an attack near or in your defending circle but on the far side from you. If the ball is on that side of the field the right back will be up to her inner and immediately this happens you must leave your right wing and move across to mark the right inner. You do not completely neglect your right wing who by now is thoroughly sick of the sight of you, you are always aware of her movements, but since she is the forward farthest away from the ball at the time it is unlikely that in such a position she can be of any great help to her colleagues. You can safely temporarily neglect her and devote your attention to the ball side of the right inner. I repeat the ball side because no matter how close you are to that right inner, unless you go across so that you are between her and the ball, and you are, in fact, nearer to the ball than she is, you might as well go and have a chat with their goalkeeper for all the good you will be doing. As soon as the attack is broken up or as soon as the play is switched over to your side and your right wing is looking dangerous again then get back to your own position, confident that the left back has returned to look after the right inner.

Now what about anticipation? This, I suppose, comes only, or at least shall we say develops, from experience. Sometimes it is more difficult than at others. For instance the unexpected

LEFT HALF

happens, or an unorthodox action is taken by an opponent. On the other hand it may be easier when the opponent is not skilful enough to hide her intentions and makes it quite obvious where she is going to send the ball long before she actually does so. Going even further on this subject she may turn out to be more clever than you think and deliberately look one way and send the ball the other.

You can't always expect to anticipate correctly—you've got to know through experience the player, the conditions and the circumstances and because, of course, you are not the other player and you cannot wholly read her mind, you can only conclude. But you can train yourself to think ahead, to think for and as others and not just for the moment and for yourself. It is a sort of very quick split second mental process which puts you in your opponent's place and cross examines you about your coming action. It is a tremendous help in any game to try and always be one move ahead. I've tried it and experimented and found it to be so. In a team game when there are times when you yourself are not directly involved there is no need to do it all the time but in a very fast game like squash, for instance, I've found that I can save energy by calculating the exact stroke, the exact moment when I shall need to use it fully and not wasting it on unnecessary movements. The sort of anticipation needed in hockey is, I think, a little bit like that. I don't mean that you become lazy minded and lazy footed, quite the opposite in fact, but that you do practise seeing ahead enough to know when you can afford to 'free wheel' and when you must pedal hard.

In all physical action there is a propelling movement and a recovery period, we can't go on fully extended all the time and it would be stupid to try, so we attempt to use both periods to the best of our advantage. I have often as a forward been chased by a player who is as fast a runner as myself and I have used this principle; I have timed my dribbling so that each time she extends herself to tackle I push the ball forward enabling me during her recovery period to recover myself. If the two actions didn't coincide I would not have the necessary extra strength and speed needed to keep the ball away from her stick.

Anticipation, of course, does not always apply to your opponents' movements but equally to your own team's actions as well. As a left half try to feel when your left back, for example, needs your help, perhaps at a free hit when all space ahead of her is blocked or when your left wing has been forced to tap the ball back to you because she has not had time to position herself correctly. It really amounts to understanding, in this case, amongst your own team.

Now for tackling; more than any other player you are in a most difficult position to tackle your particular opponent the right wing. Because she receives all her passes from her left you are marking her on that side, yet when she is in possession of the ball you have got to have sufficiently good footwork and speed to place yourself on the other side of her where she has the ball—and all this without obstructing her. There is no doubt about it that as a left half you must have very good footwork, very good stickwork and as if that isn't enough a very good turn of speed too. It's certainly a position worth fighting for. Take a look now at what I have written about the jab tackle, for this, you will find, most useful. We will assume that your opposing right wing is very fleet of foot (as she should be) and that you, chasing her as she dribbles down the wing, are forced to use an emergency stroke—the jab. Choose your moment, when she is recovering, and then make your piston-like action with all the energy you can summon—this action will be just enough if it's accurate, we hope, to push the ball out of line and to enable you to get your feet round to face her, to put your other hand back on your stick and to finish off the job. It all sounds very easy but you'll need to practise it! You'll also need to practise reversed stick tackling, trying to perfect it without any body contact to avoid obstruction. Chris Aspinwall, who has played left half for England, changed to this position from a left inner and very quickly developed into a very fine player, so if you feel like making a change of position yourself, you never know, it might be quite a good idea!

What about attacking? Well, obviously the best way you can help is by helping your own left wing. She will rely on you and her inner a great deal for the amount of work she gets in the game and if she's anything like me she won't like to be neglected. Give her the passes she needs where and how she wants them and don't over-hit them if she is near to you. If she is marked closely then use the inner and at times when your team is attacking give an occasional pass across to the right inner behind the forwards—this can be most valuable and looks so good too I always think, which oddly enough is somehow necessary to the design of the game; the delicate balance between long and short passes, between the right and the left of the field—it's the occasional stroke that seems like a long thread to link the whole pattern of the game together.

By all means have a go at shooting as well but only if you find yourself in front of your wing. If she is there then pass the ball to her and let her get on with it. At rolls-on use all the ways I have suggested in Chapter 8 and try to use them each at the right time. If you are in your defending '25' for instance it would be most unwise to use your left back unless you were absolutely sure that there was no one near enough to be of any danger, or if your wing is quick enough to see the possibility if a long roll up the side line and has indicated for it then take the opportunity quickly. Let her take the roll-on if it is very near your attacking goal line and at defending rolls-on, by the way, remember to mark on the goal side of your opponents. Free hits, again, are something which you can either waste or use advantageously. Take them quickly but accurately. Make up your mind quickly the best place to send the ball and then get on with the job. At attacking corners back up your forwards but always be aware of your non-stick side and the possibility of a clearance to your right wing. In defending corners get out as quickly as you can to the inner, if your wing is taking the hit, and try to prevent her getting in a shot at goal.

Well, that's the lot, and it's a good deal. You've got a hard task—you'll get plenty of opportunities to show your physical and mental skill but I can tell you that if you do it well you'll be very much appreciated.

CHAPTER XIV

RIGHT WING

I ALWAYS used to be one of those people who imagined that right wing was the easiest position to play on the field. That was before I tried it. I now know better. I do believe, however, that apart from the fact that any new position obviously takes time to learn and having learnt one fairly well one tends to regard it as one's own forever more, the positions on the forward line although all part of a chain of players with a common aim are specific in themselves and that a forward is right for one position much more so than another. Following on from there, I would say then, that the position of right wing is no less difficult than any other forward position but that just like other positions, it has its own difficulties, its own fascinations and its own tactics to be learnt.

All forwards must know how to get goals—that is their job. All forwards must be speedy, tacticians, opportunists as well as copy-book stylists who know how to dodge, how to dribble, who know the strokes and most of all who know how to attack—for attack they must. They must work together always realizing that success will only come if they are united, if they understand completely their respective jobs and those of their colleagues, and if they are confident in themselves and those players. Well might it be said of them 'united they stand' etc. This does not mean that they are a bunch of over-polite players falling over themselves to let the other go first—that will not get them anywhere—or who are too scared to do a solo effort because of what the others may say, or think. They must, as I said, be opportunists; they must not be greedy or selfish—the balance is the solution to the success of their role. They must think of themselves as a little team of their own, ready to interchange positions, to combine together, to always provide a constant threat by attacking.

As a right wing your most important qualities over and above all the general ones that we have mentioned will be speed, dribbling, driving and dodging.

First of all speed. You *must* be able to run fast. Where as an inside forward can get away with it by politely shouting 'yours' when she finds she is unable to get to the ball, you have no one on whom to call (other than perhaps the umpire who doggedly remains impassive). You must understand that you are there not only to be used (you hope) by your half back behind you and your inner but also to keep the ball in play. You cannot afford to take risks, so from the start get it firmly established in your mind that you intend to develop a very strong sense of determination about this business of saving balls from going over the side line and you will be surprised what a help it is. I have often, or so I thought, extended myself physically as much as I could and then found that something mentally clicked and I knew that if I tried again I would succeed—and succeed I would. So you see, the word determination, or mental effort, must be coupled with the word speed for I am sure it is of great importance.

Your speed itself, of course, is needed when you are in possession of the ball and are dribbling it down the wing. Here the faster you can go the better. Keep your ball well out in front of you, be aware of where you are going and where your opponents are and where also your other forwards are. Choose your moment to centre, get the ball in front of your left foot, keep your head well over the ball as you do and drive it hard and accurately. A good hard clean centre from a wing is a wonderful thing to see and if a goal doesn't result from it then it isn't your fault. Your passes will vary of course, and rightly so, but if it is one of these hard centres I am talking about I think you ought to aim it for the space ahead of the left inner. That is the spot where it is likely to be of most use to your forwards and of most trouble to the opposing defence. Now

PLATE XV. Rolling the ball on. Feet and stick well behind line. Bend down to it.

PLATE XVI. Hand close to ground before release.

PLATE XVII. Be ready to step on to the field of play immediately ball has been released.

PLATE XVIII. Receiving a pass from behind on the left. Feet forwards; stick indicating where ball is to be sent.

PLATE XIX. Receiving a pass from behind on the right. Again feet must be facing forwards, i.e. towards the goal you are attacking; only stick is turned to collect ball.

PLATE XX. Interception showing one-handed reversed stick fielding of the ball.

PLATE XXI. Head over ball; short back lift.

REVERSED STICK BACK PASS

PLATE XXII. Taking the ball from off your toe.

PLATE XXIII. Short follow-through.

PLATE XXIV. Notice hands apart; short back lift.

REVERSED STICK PASS TO RIGHT

PLATE XXV. Weight on the front foot throughout.

PLATE XXVI. A short, crisp stroke with little follow-through.

THE BULLY-OFF

PLATE XXVII. Feet apart either side of line: hands well apart; weight well controlled and balanced.

your other passes will depend on where you are and to whom you are passing. Most of them will take place between you and your inner, so have an understanding with her and make sure you know what she likes and that she knows what you like. Here, you will find what we call 'triangular' passing invaluable. If done correctly at the right time it is an exceedingly reliable way of getting past your opposing left half and having eliminated one defence player you are well on the way to getting that ball in the back of the net. At least you feel that progress has been made through your (in this case combined) efforts and that is what every forward should try to aim for. There is no earthly good in two forwards passing the ball neatly between them, backwards and forwards, if in doing so the position of the opposing defence has not been weakened—it is a waste of time and stickwork.

Imagine you have the ball, you start to dribble down the wing and your opposing left half advances towards you to tackle (if she doesn't then don't bother to pass). When you are sure she is close enough to you to be of no nuisance to your inner, pass the ball accurately and fairly squarely to your inner. She immediately controls it and passes it diagonally forwards back to you. You have not stopped running whilst this is going on, you have simply drawn your defence, passed, and continued running to receive the return. It is as simple as that and whilst the poor left half is turning round, to chase you, you are well on the way down the field preparing to centre. Another pass you will find yourself constantly doing is the one right across the attacking circle for your forwards to shoot. This is not easy, at least not easy to find the right place to send the ball where it will not be intercepted by the defence. If you are near the goal line there are two possibilities, either straight across the goal mouth about a yard in front of the goalkeeper (and by doing so we hope on the non-stick side of the defence facing you) or back to the edge of the circle possibly for your centre half to shoot. Don't try anything in between unless you happen to see a forward unmarked but usually it is far too crowded.

Your passing then, as I said, must be varied, sometimes long sometimes short, sometimes square, or diagonal or even back, but try to learn when you should use which—that's something you've got to find out from experience. Most of them will be drives with your hands together on the handle and a good crisp hit. I very rarely see a right wing doing push strokes or scoops—their position seems to call much more for good driving. What I do see them doing and what it is essential for them to do is to cut in on a pass to them to prevent the left half intercepting. If the ball is not going to reach you, you must be prepared to run back, gather it, run your feet round quickly (turning to the right) and dodge or pass. Here the pass might well be just a little push to your inner as she will probably not be very far away from you. Then immediately get back on the side line again ready for a return pass from her if she uses you. I mentioned dodging just now. As a right wing you will rarely use the left dodge as no one will be tackling you from your right, but a controlled push in the right dodge to your left half's non-stick side or a flick over her stick will be most valuable to you. If you discover she is too good with her reversed stick intercepting, then you must try and wrong foot her first and a slowing down and then a sudden change of pace can often beat her.

It is most important that as a wing you stay out. If you crowd in on your inner not only are you making things difficult for her but you are making it so easy for the defence to mark both of you at the same time. Do your running up and down the side line (not the five-yard line) and look dangerous enough to occupy that left half even if you aren't used by your right inner. The times when you have good reason to go in are to cut in to a ball to you which would otherwise be intercepted, or if there has been some interchanging movement amongst the forwards, or to shoot if the opportunity occurs. By this I mean if you have passed your left half and have not been challenged by the left back or if you have made a breakaway and are ahead of all your other forwards. Don't be afraid to shoot—you are a forward and your job is to make or score goals but always let someone else do it if she is in a better position than you.

One of the most important things a forward must practise is getting into the habit of having her feet always facing the way she is attacking. It is so important for a forward to be ready before she receives the ball, not to receive it and then get ready and in the meantime to be tackled and lose it. If you are anticipating a pass to you get back by all means, particularly if your defence are being hard pressed to clear the ball at all, but get back in time to be facing the right way when the ball

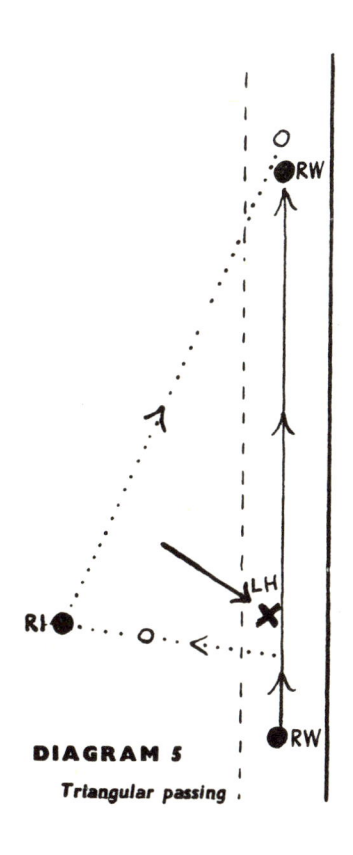

DIAGRAM 5
Triangular passing

is hit to you and better still to be *moving* when you receive it (Plates xv, xvi). You then collect it and are off—in one movement. As a right wing all your passes will be coming from your left—even if it is a pass from your left half who may be immediately behind you, see that you position yourself to receive it on your left (remember it doesn't matter if you have your feet outside the pitch if the ball is still inside the line)—and knowing this should help you to show quite clearly with your stick where you would like the ball.

There is one time when you do receive the ball from your right. I wonder if you can guess when it is? Yes, it is at a roll-on from your right half. You will probably like this right up the side line as parallel with it as possible so that you sprint on to it and gain possession before it is intercepted or before the left half tackles. Then see that you do something constructive with it—don't lose it after having the advantage of a roll-on to your side. It is difficult for a wing to do a lot with a roll-on and I personally think that inners can play much more useful parts than they do in this matter. At defending rolls-on don't leave your right half to do all the marking—she will be most grateful if you mark the opposing left wing on the defending (goal) side leaving her to go further down the field. If the roll-on is to your team and is in your attacking '25' be prepared to take it yourself, particularly if it is very close to the goal line. Your position off the pitch will mean there is a little more room in an already crowded area. So practise those rolls, with your right hand and left hand, although as the direction of the ball will in most cases be straight across the pitch at right angles to the side line it can be performed with your normal throwing hand whichever that is.

I have to mention only one more point but as usual it is by no means the least important. This is the taking of corners. Corners are awarded because of some foul or action by your opponents; they are an advantage to your team; they should result, particularly if they are short corners, in a goal. That we must all acknowledge but—and it is a very big but—no team of forwards are going to score goals, no matter how brilliant they may be, unless you can first hit the ball to them. Look at that again and then realize that you have here a tremendous responsibility. It is absolutely essential that that ball goes where you intend it to go and where the receiving forward intends it to go and that spot is one and the same place. How you send it there is your business and not hers but how it arrives is going to make all the difference in whether or not a goal is scored as a result. Practise, practise, practise—until you can send the ball to any given spot inside that circle line and only then be satisfied that you are playing fully your part in the taking of a corner. Who you hit it to we have already dealt with in the chapter on corners (Chapter 6) but remember now that it is your particular responsibility and honour to take the corner hit and make it a worthy one.

Well, I come back to my original remark—it's not easy, I'll never say it is again, but *chacun à son goût*.

CHAPTER XV

RIGHT INNER

THERE's something attractive about inside forward positions. They always have plenty to do, or should have, they are frequently the spearheads of attack and they have much more room than the other members of the forward line in which to do their dribbling and dodging and passing. These positions are for those who really enjoy all the throes of attacking and of the making and scoring of goals. Unlike wing players and centre forwards who are much more closely marked by the half backs, inners have a certain amount of freedom which calls for plenty of initiative and enterprise if they are not to waste their opportunities. They need speed and thrust in the game in addition to being able to dribble the ball well, dodge successfully, and to know when to keep the ball and when to pass it. Right inner is not an easy position but then none of them are—and you have a big responsibility because you are so much in the game. More than any other forward, I think, goals ought to come from the inside forwards—they must be essentially 'attacking' players, they must have an 'offensive' attitude all the time—otherwise they are wasting a good position.

One of the most important things to consider is, I think, positioning. You can be of so much help and you have so many opportunities and yet it can all be wasted if there is a lack of positioning, or, that is to say, a lack of understanding of how you can help. Firstly, no matter where you intend to put yourself, see that you are facing the right way. A forward with her back to the goal she is attacking neither looks nor is useful. If one has to consider when watching a forward which way she is playing then you can be sure that she is not worth watching any longer. A good forward at first glance should make it quite clear into which goal she is attacking—her whole movements, her physical and mental efforts are directed towards that goal—that is her job and that is what she must concentrate on throughout the game. So try and always be facing the way you are playing—at least with your feet for they are the important things in starting you off on that attack. Turn your body, or look over your shoulder to watch the ball, but always try to be moving forwards when you receive it so that there is no delay— you move, you gather the ball, you move—that's the sort of sequence you must aim for. This is the sort of positioning when you are receiving a pass from behind you from your defence. It will be coming either from an angle or from directly behind you perhaps, but whichever it is you must decide on which side it is best to receive it, and move so that you can do so with the minimum amount of slowing down.

Passes from your other forwards, of course, will be easier to deal with. They may even be coming towards you as, for example, when your right wing sends you a back pass from the goal line for you to shoot or similarly at a corner. All of them need collecting, or trapping, with your stick, and then dealing with intelligently without delay. Whatever the pass, whatever the circumstance, you can help so much by showing where you would like the ball. It is surprising how often good players don't do this and how much it is appreciated when they do. You cannot expect or blame your defence if the ball does not arrive where you need it if you have not done your best to indicate where you want it. So ask for it! Put your stick out on the ground either ahead of you or to the left or on the right with the blade facing the ball and then at least you have been as co-operative as you can be. Just one reminder after all this— go to meet the ball if it isn't coming just quite how you like it or not quite as fast as you had hoped. It is only a change of direction—you will still be moving when you receive it.

As a right inner you must be able to score goals and to follow up like lightning shots at goal if the goalkeeper stops them.

Anticipate the shot, if it is not your own, wait until it has been hit so that you will not be off side and then sprint with your stick down and your eyes on the ball. Your very action and the look of determination on your face should be enough to bother the goalkeeper and make her panic and perhaps mis-kick or clear it to another forward instead of to one of her own team.

We have already dealt with the taking of corners but remember if you are shooting then do so quickly, and accurately with a short back-lift of your stick and aiming at either side of the goalkeeper; if you are not then pass, equally as quickly, for a second spent in either alternative may mean that the defence are there in time or the goalkeeper has anticipated well enough to block the shot.

Now dodging. There will be plenty of opportunities and plenty of occasions when you must dodge but bear in mind that if circumstances permit to pass the ball is a far better way of eliminating a tackle. Quite often circumstances do not permit. There may be no other player better positioned than yourself, there may be no other player at all if you have made a break away run or there may not be time or space in which to pass. It all adds up to the fact that you must be able to perform at least one dodge effectively. Practise them, you may develop one more than another perhaps but get to know them all and when to use them. The key to the successful dodge, I am sure, is confidence. You must, of course, have the necessary footwork and stickwork but even so, having achieved that much, without feeling confident that you will succeed, the whole thing still remains a matter of chance instead of skill. It comes back again to this very important factor, the mental attitude, in which I am a great believer. We have discussed the dodges in Chapter 5 but of the three described there, the most likely one for you to use is the right dodge. As your left back approaches veer to the left a little, just to attract her attention in that direction, and then push the ball to the right just as her stick approaches. Remember no dodge is complete until you are re-united with the ball, that is the idea, to evade an opponent and to retain possession of the ball—so the more quickly you can meet up with that ball the other side of the left back the better. You never know when you might have to do it all over again the next second against someone else, or another dodge altogether perhaps, so be prepared. Denise Parry, England's famous forward, is a fine exponent of this dodge and is often able to do two or three in a very short space. She puts it to great use in the circle after receiving a corner hit.

Your right wing will depend on you as right inner for a great deal of her work. We have already described the triangular passing between you and her in the previous chapter. It is most effective and well worth using when the occasion arises. Keep level with the right wing if she is in possession of the ball and if you see her drawing her left half be ready for that square pass straight on to your stick. Get your left shoulder and elbow well round as you collect the ball, merely control it, don't dribble, and immediately send that long forward pass back to the wing again. If you are in possession of the ball in your defending half don't neglect the use of that long pass to the wing particularly if you know she is a fast runner and able to centre well—it is an excellent way of opening out the game and gaining ground at the same time. Watch the space too between you and your wing and remember that if you are on top of each other you are both very much more easily marked by the opposing defence as well as being useless to each other.

Get to know and to work with your left inner. Between the two of you, if you combine well, you can be most dangerous in attack. Accurate passing, switching the ball from side to side, splitting the defence, following up each other's shots—all make for successful attacking play. And use that long pass ahead across to the left wing too which also opens up the game and worries the defence. Whatever your passes, vary them, to the left and to the right, square and forward, don't hold on to the ball too long but if the way is clear then go ahead, deliberately and confidently. Be alert and moving at rolls-on and free hits and practise bullies until you are really good at getting the ball.

CHAPTER XVI

CENTRE FORWARD

THE first time I played for England—it was a touring team in South Africa in 1954—I played centre forward. I shall always remember that day. It was the second match of our tour, we had had a quick practice, at which I had played centre forward, as soon as we got off the boat at Cape Town, then a match at Kimberley at which I had cheered my team to victory from the stands and then came my first chance. I was very lucky to be there at all—I was only a territorial reserve at the time—but playing centre forward, a position comparatively unknown and certainly unpractised did not at all help the feeling I had at that moment. I was extraordinarily excited but at the same time I was very scared and felt extremely inadequate. I remember sitting on the veranda of the wonderful sports club in Salisbury beside Beryl Chapman as she put on her pads and then I remember walking out over the green turf, to the pitch. I didn't know what I was going to do, I couldn't have thought if I had tried, I just knew that I was going to try like I had never tried before. Luckily for me I scored quite early on in the match and after that I was all right. Everything went fine, I had a wonderful game and the ball just seemed to run right for me all the time. I am sure it gave me a lot of confidence afterwards and helped me a great deal. I sat in a steaming bath with Sue Hyde after the game (Sue who was later to become England's centre forward and who was playing left inner!) and we both felt very pleased with ourselves. Sue had got three goals and I had got three and we had won 7—0. We both must have looked like an advertisement for Puritan soap.

But you know centre forward doesn't always mean you are

in the limelight. Sometimes you are, but sometimes you must do a great deal of work behind the scenes, in an unobtrusive sort of way. It all depends really on your opposing centre half for she is the person who will or will not allow you to do your job to a certain degree. If she marks you really closely as she should if she is a good centre half then a great deal of your time will be spent in eluding her and by so doing occupying her and making way for the inners to go through. That is how you can help—by always appearing a potential danger even if you are not always used in the attack. You may, for example, deliberately pretend to intercept some of those cross passes from inner to inner in order to take your opposing centre half with you, and then just when she is getting used to this idea surprise her by sprinting on to the ball and bursting through with all the speed you can summon.

If, of course, your centre half is not so attentive, you have wonderful opportunities to enjoy yourself to the full. Dribbling, dodging, sometimes going through on your own, sometimes passing to the left or to the right, first time shots at goal from centres and shooting at corners will all come your way. In a way you are like your centre half in that you can do a great deal in directing the pattern of the game. If you have the ball in the centre of the field you must pass if you are going to pass at all to the left or to the right. It is you who must make the choice of side and then carry it out accurately and effectively. Sometimes it will be short just to your inner, sometimes a long one aimed at the corner flag for your wings, but which side you are going to use and how must come from you. So be decisive, get a picture of the whole game, and try and sense when the ball is needed on a particular side. By all means of course go ahead yourself too if you feel confident—remember you are the leader of the forward line and all the great centre forwards that I can think of have had this ability to sprint forward in a brilliant solo effort, just when it was needed and just when the defence felt sure that they were going to pass. Try and develop this feeling for surprise tactics for the correct balance between them and orthodox passing will be the key to your success.

As a centre forward, of course, you must know how to bully. Practise it and always think when you take up your position what you are going to do with the ball when you get it. There are various things you can do at a bully—you may perhaps have discovered others—but these are some suggestions. Practise them and vary them.

(*a*) At the end of the third tap against your opponent's stick turn the blade of your stick with a quick movement of your wrists to face ahead of you and push the ball between her feet. Whilst she is stepping back quickly get your stick to the ball again and pass immediately. Remember it is a foul to put the ball between your own feet.

(*b*) Quickly turn your stick and draw the ball towards you at the same time stepping back to avoid it going between your own feet. This is similar to the left dodge except that as your opponent is standing still it must be done even more quickly and the ball must be passed immediately before she can get her stick to it again. You need to be agile and have nimble feet.

(*c*) As your opponent's stick comes to the ball, trap it between your two sticks and then quickly lift it over her stick.

(*d*) Have an arrangement with your centre half that you will pretend to go for the ball but will hesitate at the last moment, lifting your stick so that the unprepared centre forward, expecting opposition, hits the ball straight to your centre half.

(*e*) At the end of the third tap, turn your stick over quickly to a reversed position with a quick wrist movement and flick the ball back to your centre half or for you to push to your right inner yourself.

Those are some ideas, practise them and see if you like them and if you can do any of them successfully. Remember whatever you intend to do at a bully you must stand square with your shoulders and feet to the side line and you must keep the blade of your stick quite flat throughout the bully. When you watch big matches you will probably notice how fast the players seem to bully—I know I did and thought it looked so terrific to be able to do it at such a speed, but you know it isn't the speed of the bully that matters but what you do afterwards. That is where you need the speed, after that third hit against her stick and quite often you can fool your opponent by deliberately bullying slowly making her think that she has plenty of time to do her dodge! So try it out with a partner, don't tell each other which dodge you are going to do and see who wins. Bend down to it, and have your right hand almost half way down your stick if you like but feel comfortable and agile, not stiff jointed and heavy footed (plate xvii).

This job of indicating where you are and where you want the ball is most applicable to your position as so often a centre forward tends to hide, quite unintentionally I am sure, behind her opposing centre half. She may have done the right thing and gone back for the ball when her defence are clearing but having got so far she still does not make her presence obvious. You must be aware of the fact that your defence cannot see through your opposing centre half and that you must keep moving first to one side and then to the other all the time making spaces or running into spaces to receive the ball. You may not get it, they may use someone else but at least you have been prepared.

If it does come to you, before you even receive it try and know just where your opposing players are, particularly that centre half of course. Try to have decided what you are going to do with it and try and be ready facing the way you are playing—three most important things that will improve your game beyond measure.

To sum up then, a centre forward is someone who is very much in the game whether she is leading the attack or working unobtrusively in the background, and so she must follow the game throughout so that she knows when it is balanced and running smoothly or when it is one-sided and lacking in team spirit. She must use to the full her power of distributing attacks on both sides of her, remembering that she is a member of a forward line of five whose aim is to score goals and in addition to all this she must be able to go ahead on her own, dribble, dodge and shoot with accuracy and speed. It is a most responsible and satisfying position that calls for a great deal of foresight and intelligence as well as physical skill but it is also very rewarding for those who have these qualities.

CHAPTER XVII

LEFT INNER

I LIKE this position and I can never make up my mind which I prefer, this or left wing for I have had great joy from playing both. When people ask me for my choice I am invariable stumped for an answer, I suppose it is because they are so different—there can be no comparison. It only goes to show that there can be two positions, both forward positions, both attacking positions and both in a line of five and yet still they can be immensely dissimilar and satisfying in their own particular way.

There is no doubt about it that the left inner position on the field is a most attractive one and I fail to see how any forward cannot derive enjoyment from playing in it. You have freedom to move, to receive the ball, to dodge, to dribble, to initiate attacks. You have opportunities to score, and score you must if you are playing here, to open up the game, to go through on your own, to interchange, with your centre forward or wing. It all needs intelligence, foresight, speed and skill. Why? Because you have a large responsibility to yourself and to your team and because they look to you to get goals for them and whether you do or do not depends on how you deal with the ball not only in the circle but in mid-field as well—equally as important. You don't just sit back waiting for the pass for you to shoot the goal—no forward does that—you must and are expected to play your full part in all the fetching and carrying that may have to go on and all the helping out in defence and the making of goals long before they ever end up in the back of the net. But more than any other forward you are the one I think, who must score those goals. You see you are in a most favourable position to do so. All your passes from three of your colleagues on the forward line will come to you from your right and all your passes from at least three of your defence will be from this direction and we can say then that 75 per cent of passes will be coming to you at such an angle that they reach your stick first before they reach you—an obvious advantage. You do not have to wait like the poor right wing for the ball to cross in front of her body before she can do anything with it with her stick. It should be easy for you then to put your stick out touching the ground with the blade facing towards the ball and to collect that ball as you move with the absolute minimum amount of slowing down, in fact, even to accelerate as you do so. Think of passes from your defence, perhaps the centre half or perhaps longer ones from the right back or even the right half. They will be coming from behind you, the angle varying according to your position on the field and you will have your feet facing towards the goal you are attacking and your stick on your right, slightly behind you, the blade turned to face outwards. Try to be moving when you receive them, go to meet them if they are in danger of being intercepted and curl the blade of your stick round the ball as you gather it—think of it almost as if you are protecting it, as, indeed you are! Then having got it going straight ahead, keep it close to your stick until you get rid of it and it is no longer your responsibility. That's how a forward should collect the ball—you notice next time you watch a good match and see how lovely it looks to see a beautifully controlled receiving of the ball in mid-field.

The other passes to you from your defence, from the left half or left back for example may be coming to you on your left; the same positioning applies but this time have your stick across your body touching the ground on your left and as the ball touches the blade, control it by 'giving' just a little with your stick and then instead of trying to move the ball, move your feet. I have often said that your feet must be made to work harder than the ball, well, here's an example. Trap the ball and immediately run your feet round to the left so that you have re-positioned yourself with the ball on your right ready for dribbling, passing or dodging. This is so much better if you can do it smoothly without interrupting the flow of the game than waiting until the ball has crossed in front of you and arrived on your right by which time it is quite possible that an opponent's stick has arrived there as well! Only wait if there is no one about and you are sure of being able to collect it easily. Passes which are ahead of you, of course, can be collected like this for the fact that there is a space in front, in between you and the ball, will enable you to position yourself correctly as you run on to it.

Now what about passes from you other forwards? They may be square ones, straight on to your stick or forward ones like those from the defence which you can run on to. They all need preparation and positioning for the receiving of them and they all need your attention with your hands comfortably apart on your stick, your stick feeling and looking pliable and your brain active. As a left inner I have found a forward pass ahead from the right inner a most useful pass. It looks as if it is meant for the centre forward (perhaps it is!), but if you see that there's an opportunity sprint on to it and when you collect it carry on in the same direction, which is roughly towards the right corner flag, so that you have in fact run into the right inner's position. The backs will be upset by this sudden interchanging and you will find it easy to take the ball swiftly round your opponent's non-stick side as she runs towards you and hey presto! there you are on the edge of the circle ready to shoot. It's a surprise tactic. So don't try to do it too often, otherwise it will cease to be a surprise, but take the opportunity when it comes and make the very most of it.

Remember, you've got to score goals and how you score is your responsibility. That's only one way, of course, and certainly don't try and make it the only one, otherwise your right inner will probably offer to change places for good. Scoring from the left is the real thing to master and it's difficult as I expect you know. I've found that I can do it best by a

DIAGRAM 6

Left dodge by Left inner at long corner

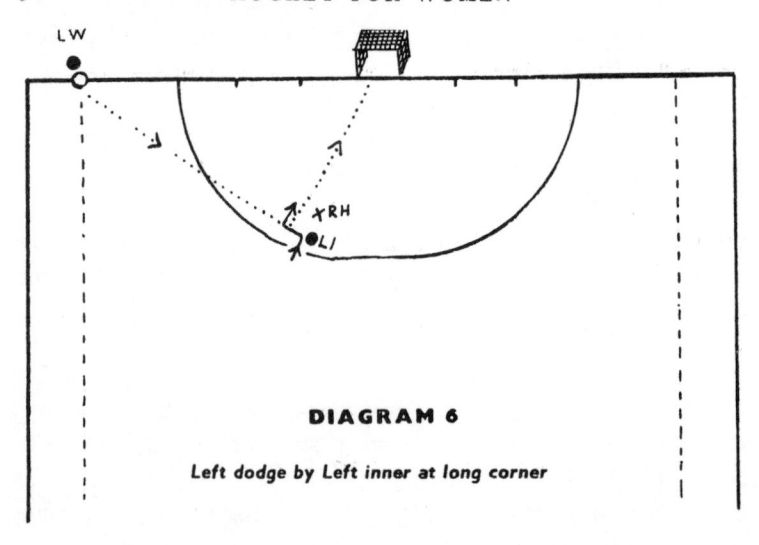

push-scoop stroke, I never seem to have time to position my body for a drive. I think if you try and develop this powerful form of shooting you will find it most valuable. Practise dribbling the ball from the twenty-five-yard line into the circle and then without altering your position at all, get your stick to the ball and push-scoop it into the goal. You aim for a spot about two feet above the ground just inside either post. The far post is probably the one where there will be most space if you can get the angle, but I've found that goalkeepers are sometimes rather neglectful of those few inches between them and the near post! So you see it must be accurate. You may be very near the goal line when you make your stroke and the angle therefore means that the possible spaces into which to put the ball are considerably lessened, so when you practise you must aim at something—it doesn't matter if it's an imaginary and invisible target as long as you satisfy yourself that you are getting somewhere near the mark. There is nothing more satisfying than scoring a goal by such means. It is controlled, powerful and most demoralizing to the opponents!

The same thing can happen at a corner. My favourite dodge

depends entirely on the defence. Defence are always coached to run out as fast as they can at a corner and that means that the right half probably will be running out as fast as she can to me. The faster she runs the better, because the easier it is to dodge. So even if I have received the corner hit in good time I wait, ready and balanced, until I see her stick almost on the ball and then pull it quickly to the left—the left dodge in fact—only a little way is necessary, as she is running so fast, and then you are free to shoot, at that far corner probably. You may have to do the dodge again against the right back who has gallantly come to the rescue, but you have all the time in the world and she is rushing hard and panicking. You may say what if they don't rush towards you? Fair enough, but then surely if they don't rush, you don't have to dodge, so you shoot straight away. The mouse won't wait for the trap door once he's got the cheese.

I haven't mentioned yet your poor left wing. I hope you don't neglect her in the game as I have done up to now, for she depends a great deal on you for the amount of work she is going to get in the game. And don't think of it in a condescending sort of way either. Get it into your head that using your wing can be one of the most useful things you can ever do as a left inner. You will have to have an understanding with each other. What she will not want you to do is to go for balls that are meant for her or to pass her a long pass ahead when you know she has just come back for a square one. Another thing she will not like you to do is to get in the way of her hard centre which is meant for the right inner, so be warned! In other words you must work together with sympathetic passing and understanding. Your left half too will join in this, for she feeds you both and should chaperone you both in attack. Be prepared for a square pass from your wing if you see she is drawing her opposing right half and then having dodged the half back send her the return well ahead of her, but whenever you can, particularly if you are in your defending half, get the ball out to your wing and send her away with a pass that is just right and just where she wants it. It may be after a hit-out, it may be after a clear once from your defence or it may be after a roll-on, but have a look where that opposing right half is and make your pass accordingly. If she is marking your wing closely then pass ahead on her non-stick side, if she has chosen to mark the space rather than the player, then use the square pass—it is as simple as that. And keep on doing it, worry them, until they don't know what to expect next.

Your passes will not always be to your wing. There are times, especially in attack, when it is most valuable to send the ball to your right. A push pass ahead of your centre forward if you see that she has the opportunity to get away from her centre half, or a diagonal pass ahead of the right inner must both be used. You can even, if you like, send a good hard drive behind them both to the right wing if you see that she is positioned for it, and be ready for the return from any of these across the circle so that you swoop on to them and shoot with a first time effort. Or if that centre doesn't come it will mean that they are going to have a crack themselves so be ready the moment you hear that hit to pounce on the goalkeeper and finish it off in case she saves it.

I mentioned earlier rolls-on and here I think you can do a great deal to help. I usually have an arrangement with my left half that I do not stand on the five-yard line at rolls-on but that I hang back and look deliberately disinterested in the whole procedure until I see that she has collected the ball and is just about to roll it and then I suddenly come to life, dart into a space on the line and she rolls the ball straight to my stick. It usually works and even when the opposition get used to the idea they never know just when and where I am going to run or even if I am going to be used at all. Quite often all this activity goes on without my being used just to add to the confusion! Having got the ball you will find your self very near the side line, so either interchange with your wing or immediately give her a pass straight up the side line. What I am trying to stress in all this is that you must not select your spot on the five-yard line, take up your position, closely accompanied by the opposing right inner on one side and the opposing right half on the other and wait. *Keep moving*, adopt whatever methods you like, but keep moving.

You know, there *is* no doubt about it, this is a most enjoyable and goal-getting position to play.

CHAPTER XVIII

LEFT WING

FINALLY, the greatest position of all! Greatest I think because it seems unique and yet I suppose one could say that about them all and perhaps I am just prejudiced. Certainly the challenge that the left wing position offers is what makes it so enjoyable to me.

Primarily the skill you must master if you are to be a successful left wing and get any enjoyment out of it at all is to be able to dribble the ball fast up the side line and *centre hard*. I cannot stress too much the importance of those last two words. To fiddle about and make delicate push passes between your inner and yourself is not the crux of left wing play. It may be necessary on occasions but it soon becomes intolerable to players and spectators alike if the ball is sent out to the left wing and she is incapable of ever getting it in again. The knowledge that, having sent it out to her, they are not likely to see it again soon discourages them from trying it any more and the whole beneficial tactic of opening out the game and thereby spreading the opposing defence has been lost. You *must* be able to centre the ball hard and you *must* be able to do it at speed. A wing is a fast player and if she isn't able to run fast she shouldn't be playing wing, for her job is to gain ground up the sideline and to provide openings for her team to score. Hence her two most important roles: (i) to speed up the attack by gaining ground as quickly as possible up the wing and (ii) to provide at the end of that run openings for goals from her fellow forwards.

Now, on analysing her first role a little further it is obvious that en route up the side line the left wing will meet with obstacles—namely the right half marking her. This is where the push passing to the left inner comes in. It is the triangular passing that we have described in Chapter 14. The left wing is approached by the opposing right half. She waits until she is sure the right half is near enough to be unable to mark the left inner as well and then makes her accurate square push pass straight to the stick of her left inner. Whilst the right half is re-positioning the left inner has controlled the ball and pushed or driven it ahead for the left wing—still running at top speed please note—to collect and centre hard. The same thing may happen if the right back comes to tackle, but by then it is usually time to centre the ball anyway. The angle of these centres will be determined, of course, by the positioning of the opposition in the first place, and secondly by your own position. Generally speaking it is right to get your centre across, perhaps for the right inner, early on, soon after you have crossed the centre line. The attack will be on your side so that the opposing left back may well be standing quite deep, but you must notice where she is and send your centre either ahead of, or on to, the stick of the right inner. Then too, there is the centre half to be avoided and you must try and aim your centre out of her reach. The faster you have accelerated at the beginning the more likely you are to get in front of her and avoid any likelihood of her intercepting. The other type of hard centre you will have to do, either because of late passes out to you or lack of opportunities to centre, is when you find yourself getting very near to the goal line. Here with nimble footwork you must get right round the ball and your centre of course will be square, or even back to the edge of the circle for your centre half following up her forwards, to shoot. If there is a gap in front of the goal send it hard along straight across the circle about two yards in front of the goalkeeper—this can prove to be a most successful pass.

To centre the ball to your right at speed therefore is something you must practise. The important thing to remember is to let the ball get behind you before you attempt the stroke. If it is to be done at speed you will find that you cannot get your feet and hips right round in the normal

DIAGRAM 7

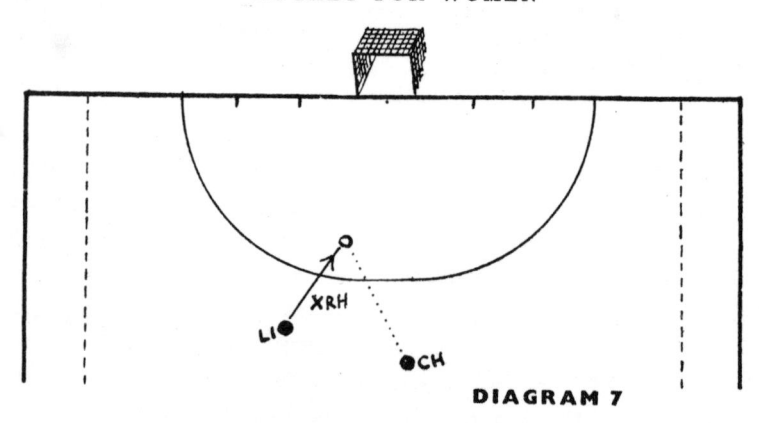

Passing to the space at a free hit

position for driving, so that there must be considerable twist of the upper part of your body from the waist in order to get your left shoulder pointing in the direction in which you intend to hit the ball. You will sometimes have little time to make the stroke so you must be able to make your centre off either foot. Practise it slowly at first, only increasing the speed when you know you are hitting the ball well.

Only on good fast grounds can you use a push pass to anyone else but your left inner. If you have strong wrists and are able to push the ball accurately and far then this is a good stroke to mix with your hard drives. There is little preparation to the stroke and it is therefore a time-saver and can also be used in an emergency if you have not time to get round, put your hands together and drive the ball. The essence of a push stroke is its accuracy and most of your push passes, therefore, will be aimed at the stick of a player.

Now passes to you. Unlike any other player on the field you are the only one to receive all your passes on your right. Even those that come from directly behind you from your left half you must position yourself, if necessary, with your feet outside the side line, to receive them on your right. A left wing very, very rarely has the ball on her left—her every action takes place on her right and she develops what one might call literally a one-sided game since all her efforts are concentrated on dealing with the ball on that side of her—to and from her.

Only at rolls-on do you ever look to your left and then you must get on the outside of the ball as quickly as possible—the second the ball has crossed over the side line at the roll. So the receiving of balls then should be one of your easier jobs; they all reach your stick first before they reach you and you should therefore be able to collect and control them quickly whilst on the move and keep your feet well out of the way at the same time. They will be coming from all angles; some well ahead which you must spring on to with great acceleration, some square and straight to you which will need stopping first in order to control them before you start your sprint up the wing; and some even behind you which means anticipation on your part, a quick run back, still on the outside of the ball, to collect it and save it from going off the side line. Wherever you are, whatever passes are given to you, some bad, some good, you are there to keep the ball in play and by not doing so you may have lost an opportunity for your team to score. This is a great responsibility for you; other players can leave it and politely shout 'yours'—you have no one on whom to fall back and you must develop a great sense of determination and concentration about the job of saving balls from going off the pitch.

You will find it so much easier to do if you keep right out on the side line. From that position not only do you allow yourself and your left inner more space in which to work and thereby more space to be marked by your opposition, but you are able to be aware of your exact position and judge your movements more accurately using the side line as a guide. Your left inner, too, will not thank you for crowding in on her, for you then become useless to her and at the same time make it so easy for the opposing right half to mark both of you. So be warned and keep right out! This does not mean, of course, that you never have to tread the sacred turf beyond the five-yard

DIAGRAM 8

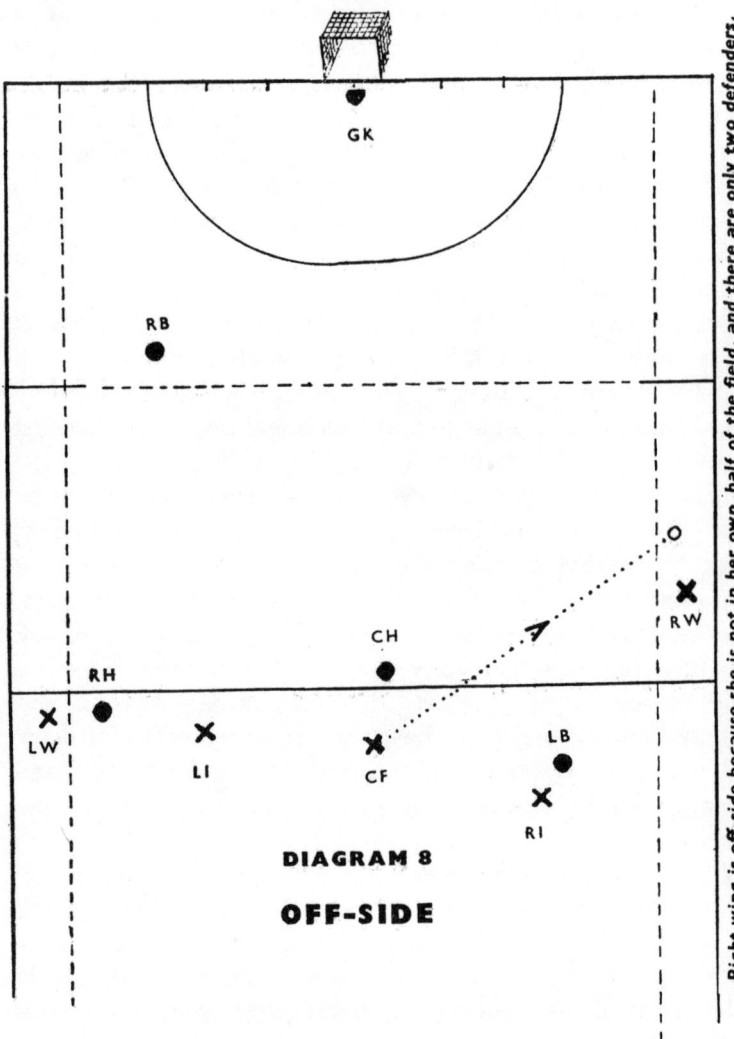

OFF-SIDE

Right wing is off-side because she is not in her own half of the field, and there are only two defenders, not three, between her and the goal when the ball was hit to her

line. There are many occasions when you will have to. There may be a forward pass to your left inner who is not up with the forward line and you must notice this and sprint on to the ball in her place, or similarly, if the pass is meant for you, but is coming too slowly, you must always be prepared to go to meet it in order to avoid interception by the defence. Don't be scared to go in and don't be scared to interchange completely with your left inner, or with any of your forwards if you like. A surprise tactic like this can often temporarily upset a defence who are stale with orthodox marking of man to man. But make sure that you know what you are doing and that you carry out your surprise tactic according to plan! To dither here and there merely results in a bewildered muddle on your forward line, but a darting run in, a crisp pass out to your left inner, now on the wing, or a cross pass to your right wing and then back to your place again is both enterprising and successful and quite refreshing to watch.

As left wing, of course, you are a forward and therefore must score goals, but don't worry if your chance doesn't come and don't hang on to the ball too long in the belief that it will come. Remember the old axiom that if there is someone better positioned than yourself to score, then pass to her making sure, of course, she is not off-side. Sometimes there will not be, or you may have broken away with a solo run and then is your chance to shoot. I invariably shoot with a push-scoop stroke, developed from the acute angle from which I quite often find myself scoring. I believe there is no better shot from such a position but if you have made a breakaway and are by yourself in front of goal then a good hard drive with your hands together to the corner of the goal is as good as anything.

Your second responsibility is corner hitting. You must realize that fifty per cent of the chances of scoring from the corner rest on your shoulders. Not even brilliant forwards can score from corner hits that are mis-hit or badly placed or bounce up to them like tennis balls. But they have a very good chance if the ball travels to them smoothly and quickly and arrives just where they want it, to be stopped and hit without delay. So see that you can hit your corner hits accurately and well and what happens after that is not your fault. And remember, too, to run back on-side immediately afterwards. You will probably have some arrangement with your forwards as to whom you are to hit the ball and in which order, and this is a good idea but like all pre-arranged tactics be prepared to adapt them if they are not proving successful. If, for instance, one particular forward is seeing the ball well or is constantly unmarked use her again and again until you see the opposition are wise to your ideas and then is the time for surprise tactics!

As a left wing you are a forward and attacking player, but your defence when hard pressed will need all the help you can give them. Tackle back whenever you can, and go back to receive passes from them out of your defending circle. At free hits and hit-outs particularly you can make yourself useful by going right back for a square hit from your left back. Time your movement so that you and the ball arrive at the same spot together and do not take up your position waiting for the ball making it quite obvious to your opposing right half who immediately comes up to mark you.

Have an arrangement with your left back that although you are not there you are quite ready! On the other hand, willing as you are to help in defence, do not muddle your own left half. She will thank you for marking your opposing right wing at free hits from the opposition, but in general play if your left half is there and has everything under control she will want you up the wing to pass to more than anything else. The two of you must combine always and a back pass from you to her may be enough to organise the attack into a most successful movement.

Just a word about dodging. It always gives a player a great thrill to elude a tackle skilfully. The left dodge is the one for you (see Chapter 5) and if you can confidently avoid defence players as they come to tackle and then pass the ball in for someone else to shoot you have been worth more than your weight in gold. You may not have been the actual scorer, but your efforts have made possible the success by eliminating the defence players who came to tackle you. It is well worth while practising your left dodge and there are times when you must use it but if you become proficient in it, like everything else—don't overdo it! Try and fox the opposition by varying your dodges as often as possible.

As left wing I have had many enjoyable games. I hope you will too.

CHAPTER XIX

EQUIPMENT

THE following notes about your equipment and uniform may be helpful.

STICKS

1. Your stick must comply to the rules, viz., it must not weigh more than 23 oz., it must be able to pass through a 2 in. ring, and it must not have any dangerous splinters or sharp edges. It is interesting to note that an umpire may prohibit play with a stick that does not comply with the rules.

2. A stick should be well weighted in the head. It is impossible to hit a heavy ball with a light-headed piece of wood with no 'body' to it and even beginners' sticks should be well balanced in this way to facilitate a pendulum-like action in their swing.

3. A stick should be well-sprung, comfortable to hold and manipulate, and *just* long enough to swing easily without hitting the ground. It is better to err on the short side rather than to have a stick that is too long. One can always progress to greater lengths, as I did, but it is impossible to play with a stick that does not permit a natural easy straightening of the arms when driving the ball.

4. A stick should have no knots in the wood and the grain of wood should follow the curve.

5. There are still English headed sticks on the market, but now that there is much more reversed stick play in the game today and, in general, a more flexible manipulation of the ball, an Indian headed, or semi-Indian, stick is the better choice. They are still, however, badly made and many are stiff and ill-balanced. Get one with some weight in the head and one that feels reasonably pliable and is well-sprung. A semi-Indian stick may give some players more driving power.

FOOTWEAR

1. Footwear should first and foremost provide a good firm grip on the ground and be well fitting and comfortable.

2. Footwear, either boots or shoes, must not have any metal spikes or projecting nails; an umpire may forbid the wearing of such footwear.

3. Boots and shoes should not be too heavy or restrict ankle movement but at the same time provide correct support to the foot.

4. Boots and shoes may be made of canvas or leather with either rubber or leather bars and studs.

5. Many players prefer to wear shoes similar to the lightweight shoes used by footballers. There are many varieties on the market but as most of our hockey in this country is played on heavy grounds it is advisable to have studs of some depth which will afford a good grip. For hard pitches rippled soles or interchangeable studs are available.

UNIFORM

1. Uniform must be either a skirt, a tunic or a divided skirt, and must not be more than 7 inches off the ground when kneeling.

2. With this must be worn either long or three-quarter length stockings.

3. No player is allowed to wear any dangerous brooch or metal clips that might harm other players and an umpire may prohibit the wearing of such articles.

4. A shirt or blouse should be of practical design, long enough to remain tucked in at the waist if worn with shorts or skirts and allowing freedom of movement.

5. A goalkeeper is allowed to wear trousers and should be careful that, whilst her comparatively static position often calls for more protection from the cold, she does not hamper her movements with heavy or tight garments.

6. Footballer's shin pads that slip inside socks often give confidence as well as protection.

7. It is a good idea to have a pair of good leather palmed gloves for use in wet weather when stick handles, particularly those with rubber grips often get very slippery.

THE BALL

The ball, according to the rules, shall be covered with white leather similar to a cricket ball, weighing between $5\frac{1}{2}$ oz. and $5\frac{3}{4}$ oz. and the circumference shall be not more than $9\frac{1}{4}$ in. Provided the size and weight is the same a plastic ball may be substituted for leather.